Leading through Chaos

Leading through Chaos

Ten Strategies for School Leaders during Crises

Lisa Leali

ROWMAN & LITTLEFIELD
Lanham • Boulder • New York • London

Published by Rowman & Littlefield
An imprint of The Rowman & Littlefield Publishing Group, Inc.

4501 Forbes Boulevard, Suite 200, Lanham, Maryland 20706
www.rowman.com

86-90 Paul Street, London EC2A 4NE, United Kingdom

Copyright © 2022 by Lisa Leali

All rights reserved. No part of this book may be reproduced in any form or by any electronic or mechanical means, including information storage and retrieval systems, without written permission from the publisher, except by a reviewer who may quote passages in a review.

British Library Cataloguing in Publication Information Available

Library of Congress Cataloging-in-Publication Data

Names: Leali, Lisa, 1977– author.
Title: Leading through chaos : ten strategies for school leaders during crises / Lisa Leali.
Description: Lanham, Maryland : Rowman & Littlefield, 2022. | Includes bibliographical references. | Summary: "Leading through Chaos supports a new leader struggling to understand how to identify and manage chaos while moving a school or district to a new and more focused reality"—Provided by publisher.
Identifiers: LCCN 2022025500 (print) | LCCN 2022025501 (ebook) | ISBN 9781475867053 (cloth) | ISBN 9781475867060 (paperback) | ISBN 9781475867077 (epub)
Subjects: LCSH: Educational leadership—United States. | School administrators—United States. | School management and organization—United States. | School crisis management—United States.
Classification: LCC LB2805 .L3464 2022 (print) | LCC LB2805 (ebook) | DDC 371.2/011—dc23/eng/20220707
LC record available at https://lccn.loc.gov/2022025500
LC ebook record available at https://lccn.loc.gov/2022025501

Contents

Foreword	vii
Preface	ix
Acknowledgements	xix
Introduction	xxi
Chapter 1: Spot the Storm	1
Chapter 2: Chase the Storm	13
Chapter 3: Provide an Accurate Forecast	27
Chapter 4: Bring Everyone Along on the Yellow Brick Road	37
Chapter 5: Wear Your Ruby Slippers with Pride	47
Chapter 6: Confront the Lions, Tigers, and Bears	61
Chapter 7: Rely on Your Brain, Your Heart, Some Courage, and a Lot of Hard Work	71
Chapter 8: Laugh, Even When the Wicked Witch Is on Your Tail	79
Chapter 9: Share Your Kansas Stories	89
Chapter 10: Celebrate Before You Reach the Emerald City	99
Chapter 11: Realize Oz Is About More Than Just the Wizard, It's About the Journey	105
Chapter 12: "Remember, there's no place like home"	109
Bibliography	113
About the Author	115

Foreword

If you are looking to be captured within the first sentences of a leadership book, you've just opened the pages to one of your new favorite books. If you are also a huge fan of the Wizard of Oz, get ready for this book to hook your heart with its imagery, examples, and connections from one of the greatest books and movies of all time to the reality of the leadership world that many of us are living in daily.

Leading Through Chaos is designed to help new leaders into the field; however, the reality is that every educator will benefit from reading this book. Not only does Leali capture leadership challenges through very practical, organized, and thoughtful reflections, she also does an exquisite job of pointing out very tangible and realistic steps that every leader should take in their organizations to improve education for all students.

The idea that we have been "leading through chaos" as educators is felt from every stakeholder in our organizations. This book enables us to see that leadership is about teams who can work to create spaces that encourage and celebrate educators to be their best, every day, for students. Not only does it address the realistic challenges that we all face in our lives, but it also encourages us to create pathways of success for our students and ourselves.

The mirror image of the analogies from Wizard of Oz to the work in the field of education will resonate with educators across the country as they read every chapter filled with vibrant and reflective connections. Leali does a beautiful job of outlining the storm that we face in education and how we will continuously be chasing the storm of barriers and challenges ahead of us. But then she quickly leads into hope, optimism, with a sense of realism, and a focus on how we can be more transparent in our communication.

Every educator can benefit from a realistic text that not only relates to the work that we do every single day, but also brings us a human element while encouraging and focusing on the importance of being transparent in our communications. One of the best takeaways of this book is the encouragement of self-reflection for ourselves as individuals. Leali calls upon readers to know and reflect on ourselves, while we wear our ruby slippers with pride and lead through the chaos.

Finally, *Leading Through Chaos* takes us on a journey to confront the lions, tigers, and bears, and addresses one of the most important challenges that we all face—figuring out how to maximize our time. Through real and practical ideas of how we can be better, we then are transported into the idea of finding humor and enjoyment within our lived chaos and encouraged to share our stories to make our profession better.

In the end, *Leading Through Chaos* is a beautiful representation of our journey as educators and will leave you reminiscing about one of the greatest books and movies of all time while reflecting on the challenges of our work. In the end, readers will feel compelled to go out and make our profession better, realizing it's always more about the journey and our impact on education than the chaos.

Dr. Courtney Orzel
Associate Director of Professional Development
Illinois Association of School Administrators

Preface

"If we walk far enough," said Dorothy, "I am sure we shall sometime come, to some place."

—*The Wonderful Wizard of Oz*

Becoming a school or district leader is a lot like becoming a parent. If it is something you *want* to do, you prepare for it before it happens. You do your research, enroll yourself in some classes, find the right tools, and you seek the experts to help guide you. Then, when it finally happens you are joyful and excited by your new role in life! There are nerves too, but in a good way. You set out to do the right things, the things that drove you to become a parent, or a leader in the first place. You set out on a journey with the ones you are leading and hope and plan for the very best outcomes for all of you.

Sometimes when you set out on that journey as a new leader or a new parent, it becomes clear very quickly that all the work you have done has not actually prepared you for this new vocation. The classes, the tools, the strategies, the experts. They are all there in your mind, or on call when you need them, but the people you are working with, those you are leading every day, are full of surprises. Whether they are your children or your colleagues, nothing fully prepares you to become *that* leader, the leader *these people* need. A lot of the learning and preparation happens "on the job."

When one decides to try the profession of educational leader and is actually chosen to lead in a school or district, there is a great responsibility that comes with making that commitment. The weightiest responsibility often feels like the one you have to your students. They are the reason that many choose this path in the first place. For those who decide to lead after working as a teacher or other staff member in a school this is often the most salient responsibility, too.

Often these types of leaders decide to take on leadership after much consideration of what they *think* educational leadership is like, based on what they have seen from their "seat on the bus." Sometimes, these folks believe that they will think more about students than others they have seen in leadership positions. Sometimes, they find that they are having to defend the decision to enter educational leadership to their colleagues for that very reason. They are told by their friends and peers that school leaders lose their connection to kids and they are asked why anyone would want to do that job.

The educators who overcome those conversations, who decide that they will be a different kind of leader and set their mind to finding a position in educational leadership, begin to prepare for their new career with these thoughts and intentions in mind. As they take their classes, do their internship hours, learn through projects and proposals, they do this with a lens of a student-focused school leader who will be ready to sift through all the "meaningless" work of a leader (meaningless from the perspective of the positions they have held before) and ensure that students and their learning and growth remain at the center of their attention.

In many cases, new and veteran leaders *can* maintain that focus on students. Upon being hired for a new position, a new leader can often come in ready to listen carefully to the needs of their new organization and think carefully and thoughtfully with their teams about how to make improvements that will result in better outcomes for students. They can move slowly at the beginning, asking the right questions and building strong relationships so that when things inevitably drift away from a focus on students, they can use all the strategies they have been taught in their preparation and the relationships they are developing, to be clear about their expectation that students will be their (and everyone else's) focus and that all efforts must align to better results for the students.

However, sometimes when a new leader begins in their new role and starts to ask all the good questions and listen, they find that not only are students *not* the focus of the organization, the students are actually attending school in a place that is entirely engulfed in chaos that is many times centered squarely on the adults and their needs. Redirecting conversations toward a student-centered focus isn't even possible because the educators in this environment are so frustrated, scared or angry that they will not engage in any conversation that seeks to remind them of their purpose. The collective chaotic energy of these places has everyone's brains hijacked and there is a general loss of the ability to think strategically and carefully or even to be self-aware or reflective on one's own thoughts or actions in relationship to students and student outcomes.

The questions that this book intends to explore are:

- Where does one begin to identify the signs of this kind of chaos as a new leader in a new school or district?
- What specifically happens to new leaders when they step into a leadership position in a time of unanticipated chaos?
- How does a new leader lead through that chaos effectively and with their emotional and mental health intact so that they might continue to lead successfully once the chaos has passed?

Time for strategic planning, slow conversations, gradual trust-building is just not there in this type of chaotic situation. The cornerstones of chaos and crisis will disrupt any leader's plans for a strategic and thoughtful entrance. Chaos will quickly envelop every conversation and distractions will take over. Often there are signs of trauma everywhere you look. But sometimes they are hidden and only discovered in moments of high emotions, like fear or anger. When chaos is the norm, triggers are everywhere, for everyone in the organization.

A new leader in a chaotic environment can find herself in discussions which are passionate, raw and full of a desperation that are difficult to analyze and assess and ultimately to process and support. A new leader may become engaged in conversations that are full of hidden agendas and history, designed to give her a perspective on the current situation that only reflects a small part of the organization's, or that individual's needs. Sometimes there is only armor. New colleagues have steeled themselves and are afraid to let any vulnerabilities show through to their new leader. There are oftentimes competing interests, competing priorities, and a changing landscape that also make it difficult to create an effective plan and stick with it.

New leaders in these types of situations may quickly find themselves asking these questions:

- Who can I trust?
- Who can answer my questions?
- What if there are no answers?
- What if I do something wrong?
- What if no one agrees on what has been done in the past or how we should move forward?
- How can I avoid looking stupid and inexperienced?
- Lots of people have done this job before and have been ok, why is this so difficult for me?

Organizational crisis and chaos can be preceded by many different types of events. It can develop internally, from situations like:

- leadership and staff turnover
- lack of or inaccurate documentation and systems
- unethical practices
- lack of trust

Or, an organization can find itself in chaos and crisis from external factors, some of these examples might include:

- economic downturns
- newly emerging competitors
- a global pandemic

Either way, or if the organization is experiencing a combination of both internal and external factors, if a new leader takes the helm of an organization experiencing crisis and chaos, she will quickly need to assess and understand her current reality and implement strategies to weather the storm and ultimately move the organization toward more calm, more normalcy and a collective vision for the future. She will need to do this in a way that preserves her ability to lead in the future as well, once the storm of chaos has started to move on.

The COVID-19 crisis was a challenge in dealing with chaos for new leaders *and* veteran leaders alike. The constantly changing health and educational guidance, technology challenges, and social and political unrest made school and district leadership feel like running in quicksand. For new leaders though, those who stepped into new positions in the fall of 2020, one of the most challenging aspects was having no relationships or history with the folks they were about to work with, and having to develop a plan to get teachers and students back in school at a time of utter panic in many communities around the United States and beyond. Without background or context, without knowing the community and the constituents, there was absolutely no trust. There were only extremely high levels of anxiety and unfortunately in many instances, not a focus on what students really needed, which was calm, safety and as much normalcy as possible.

Add to this any leader's own personal circumstances, learning to cope with the new pandemic reality and the uncertainty of how to complete even routine daily tasks for themselves and their loved ones, and it was a recipe for a great deal of personal stress and anxiety and many, many sleepless nights. Many even experienced and successful educational leaders were exhausted upon waking up in the morning and used every ounce of their energy to simply hold their communities, staff and Boards together, while simultaneously struggling to keep moving in their own personal lives. For those who were new leaders, the loneliness of this new position was unprecedented.

This book may be *one* companion during the loneliness that wraps around leaders in chaotic times and places. The kind of isolation that a new leader finds herself in can be debilitating and sometimes paralyzing with chaos swirling around them. This intense loneliness can unfortunately lead to self-gaslighting where the leader does little else but question her own mind and interpretation of events, people and outcomes. By supporting new leaders with some validating realities of chaos and crisis, perhaps that kind of self-doubt might be suppressed and overcome.

COVID-19 was not the first nor the last time that schools and school districts will find themselves in chaos. Public education is facing crises in every corner of our work. The current narratives about schools and teachers using their platforms to "indoctrinate" students are not new, however, they are rearing their heads at a time when social media is the main vehicle for the information campaign and as our political landscape is more divided than ever before.

The speed at which chaos can be created by social networks around these issues is staggering. One comment made on one online platform can be seen by thousands within minutes. Yes, schools have been under attack before, but the battles have never been waged with such lightening speed that amplifies any voice, even the most violent. The time for leaders to slow down and think is becoming more scarce, especially when the leaders themselves are also the focus of intense public scrutiny.

I have been a leader in these types of situations. Having worked for over 20 years in public education in different roles, (elementary teacher, building administrator, instructional coach, coordinator, director, and superintendent) schools, districts and for many different superintendents, I have unfortunately encountered the kinds of chaos that can transform a school or district into a place that is ineffective at best, and scary at worst. The purpose of writing this book is to provide a guidebook that may give insights to a new leader that her program of study did not provide and save her from burning out in a place like this before she even gets a chance to see her fire bring light to others.

Sometimes when an organization is in chaos, a new leader is hired specifically for that purpose. The interview process accounts for leadership skills which can address the pressing issues. These leaders are selected because of their experience or skill set in dealing with similar situations. As long as the interview committee knows what kind of crisis needs managing, there can be pointed questions and discussion about strategy and skill set of the potential leader. The candidates can describe the strategies they might employ and be given an opportunity to describe similar situations they have been in so that the selection committee can make a solid decision.

Sometimes though, the crisis comes immediately after the hiring process or worse yet, the selection committee knows little to nothing of the crisis that the organization is or has been facing. The committee might proceed to hire an inexperienced leader, who may show great potential and passion, but who has not experienced anything like what she is about to face. This book is for these situations.

The skills and strategies described in this book are offered through the lens of someone humbled by multiple chaotic experiences which caused her to feel isolation and loneliness, self-doubt, severe anxiety, and stress but which fortunately, ultimately led to much new personal learning, true insight and tremendous growth as a leader, mother, daughter, sister, friend, etc.

This book can only be *one* companion on the journey of a new leader, because in truth, in no way should any of the strategies and concepts presented here take the place of leaning on one's colleagues and collaborating with friends in the field. *It takes strength of character to reach out for help when you find yourself in chaos*. In fact, it is the opposite of weakness. Your formal leadership preparation did not focus on this type of experience. Your leadership toolbox may be full, but perhaps not with the right tools. Finding your people within the organization, finding other colleagues in your position, finding experts in other disciplines, finding more and different tools and resources, and truly connecting with others (especially your loved ones) while you are leading and living through chaos is not easy, but it is so worth it for you and your organization.

The wealth of knowledge and experience that a new leader can gain just from reaching out to friends and other leaders who have extensive, or even minimal experience cannot be matched. Kindness, respect, support, and laughter in these leadership circles can be abundant and can literally change your trajectory as a leader in the midst of the chaos and beyond.

Although this is a book for school leaders, many of the concepts discussed are based in social science research and not educational research. Leaders in all fields need this kind of information about human behavior to influence their work. The study and application of this kind of information, can lead to substantial positive changes for individuals and organizations alike and the application of it is broad and transformational.

Social science research and the applications of those findings can change the world, one individual at a time. Learning about one's own mind and the minds of others is necessary and strategic work in the life of a leader. It should be required in every course on educational leadership. For that reason, throughout the book, social science researchers are highlighted in order to lead the reader to a deeper study of the concepts presented here. Those highlighted are powerhouses of knowledge and connection and more importantly they are real people who share how this research directly impacts their lives, relationships, successes, etc.

However, this *is* a book for educational leaders and therefore, the works of educational leaders and practitioners are also presented throughout this text. These works will support the application of the concepts into the more practical aspects of working in schools and districts today. Again, many of the concepts explored here can be found in educational literature that has been around for decades. It is the hope that re-presenting these concepts will lead some folks to more practical integration of them into their daily leadership journey, or to reflect on how they are utilizing the strategies already.

This book is written from the perspective of a cisgender woman who identifies as a woman. The pronouns she/her are used to describe leadership behaviors throughout this piece and pronouns he/his are used to indicate support positions. That is intentional. It is important for women and anyone who identifies in that way, to see reinforced in print that women can and should be leading others and can do it successfully.

Although most educators continue to be females, most educational leadership positions are still occupied by males or those who identify that way. Many young, female leaders in education feel the sting of the imposter phenomenon for this reason. Agonizing over their contributions, or lack thereof. Questioning their own abilities. Through the study and application of social science, especially the research rooted in the study of women and women leaders, female leaders can learn to take control of their own thoughts and behaviors which can ultimately change everything. Attention to human behavior and healthy leadership practices can sometimes be the most effective way to proactively make you and the organizations you lead more "chaos proof." Women have done this and they can do this.

This book intends to assure young leaders, specifically young women, that they can be tremendously impactful in any leadership position, even as new leaders in chaos. Leadership of others is a gift and a great responsibility. At its best, one will be grateful for the opportunity to influence, develop and be a part of a team that will do wonderful things together in service of a common goal. At its most difficult, being a leader can make one wonder if there is any purpose to your work at all or if you have made any difference to the people you serve. But as I often reflected in the early and difficult days of motherhood, many people have done this well. Many young people have done this well. Many young women have and can do this well.

Many may read this publication later and point out missteps in the author's own leadership journeys that haven't made themselves apparent yet (and some that have). There may be a time when some people who read this book will stop here, and think that ultimately while she may have tried to use all of the strategies, the outcome didn't turn out the way she thought it would or planned for. This would not be surprising.

Leadership is not a destination, it is a journey that starts long before one's first formal leadership position. Leading others is full of twists and turns and ups and downs. On this type of roller coaster, it isn't surprising that people reach out to connect with others to feel safe and grounded. The strategies contained here are really about that type of connection, in the end. They are about connection to oneself, to others, and to the truest form of the work that matters in education—our service to students and communities. When one connects with others, though, there is no way to predict how that will go. Education is a business of humans.

Leadership is a special and dangerous business in any arena, though. Reflection and publication are, as well. Confronting in one's own mind, insights, failures, and successes is scary. Formally and informally putting yourself "out there" to share your thoughts could be the scariest thing anyone will ever do. Sharing opens the doors to criticism, reproach, and rebuttal. Human brains aren't actually designed or equipped to handle and respond to the amount of "feedback" we get on anything we put online or in public right now. But, sharing also opens the door to connection, learning, and shared experience. If we can learn from those who learn from us, then all of us will be better off.

The hope is that this book resonates with anyone who chooses to take the time to read it, or at least causes one to pause and think about their own strategies for leading and living through chaos. If it inspires a book (a podcast, an article . . .) with contradictory viewpoints, all the better. Learning from others is one of the greatest gifts that life has to offer, this type of learning can never be taken away and it will be the only thing that will ever be ours to give away to others.

Being a new parent feels chaotic for a while. Every day is a reinvention of yourself, your home, your routines. The new role causes you to reflect on who you are and it truly turns your world upside down. However, years into the job, old routines are stabilizing and new routines and traditions are initiated together when the need arises. The home reflects the family. It can be a welcoming, well-functioning, dynamic, and sweet place for everyone to connect and launch from every day together if that is the goal. Being a parent will never be without struggle, but the family that navigates those struggles together and with their values intact and shining like a flashlight ahead of them will always fare better.

The hope for any organization should be no different. Every day, leaders and teams can work together to create a space that feels right for everyone and a place where everyone can be at their best, every day. They have to strive collaboratively to make sure that students are the focus, the light. They can work together, sometimes through tremendous change and chaos, to ensure everyone feels safe and valued. Through this work, leaders and their teams can actually emerge from times of uncertainty stronger than they were before and doing their best for students, their families and their communities, every single day.

Acknowledgements

To my family of origin, those who are here, those who are gone and those we have added to our group intentionally over time, you have brought to my life a richness of experience, a history and a network of love and support that I couldn't imagine my life without. Those experiences have prepared me for so many aspects of complex and chaotic leadership and life (personally and professionally) and I am so grateful to all of them. Frank and Pat, Frank, Jr., Doug, Suzanne, Brian and Dorothy, Sean, Mike, Michael, Niko and Becky, Zachary and Lexi, Anabelle and Corbin, Ruth and John, Johnny and Allison, Jessica, Andrew and Theodore, Nicole and Dalton, Jimmy, Paul and Karyn, Abby, Emily, Ben, Dave and Deonna, Grace and Nathan, I love you.

My friends and colleagues who have held up a mirror, hung in during tough times, been honest, true and loyal partners in my life and who have encouraged me many times to move forward in my journey even when I didn't think I had anything to offer to anyone. These are my people. Their day-to-day, on-call support gets me through tough times and they celebrate with me when things are wonderful: Meg Rincker, Laura Collins, Tracy and Michael Crowe, Karen Maturo, Sarah Thorn, Brad Goldstein, Nick Brown, Zuica Donev, LeViis Haney, Howard Bultinck, the Lake County Superintendents Association in Illinois, you all know I could not do all the things without you.

Finally, my children, Ryan, Gigi, and Ava, I hope you always remember that the only career I would ever leave you for every day is one that helps other children. You are my every true joy and the only pain that actually stings is when you are hurting. Please don't ever forget how much of my heart you take up. That would be 100% (even though you know I'm not great at math).

Thanks to Lucy, too. You are actually the best dog. No question about it.

Introduction

"What a world, what a world."

—The Wicked Witch

In the late 1970s and early 1980s, movies were *not* on demand. The television couldn't be paused or recorded. No one had a magic box that let people rent shows from the couch, or even a store down the block to rent videos. Most people didn't even have VCRs in their home. If you're thinking about what a VCR is right now don't worry, it doesn't actually matter (although you might find it interesting if you decide to Google it).

At that time, movies were at the movie theater (most of the time) and if a family was home watching TV, a small child was often designated as the remote control. They were often the shaper of aluminum rabbit ears to indulge the whims of older brothers, sisters, parents and neighbors. Children today would not believe what folks had to do sometimes to make sure that they had a "signal" in the house so they could watch anything on the *seven* TV channels that they *may* have had.

Special movies and TV shows only came on once or if you were lucky, twice a year. Classics like The Sound of Music were "appointment television" in many houses. Families would read the TV schedule in the newspaper (the paper one, that got your fingers dirty from the ink) and they might pop popcorn on the stove and sit around a color television in the house, if they had one, to watch the movies that were beloved by so many. One of these family favorites was and continues to be, the Wizard of Oz (Fleming 1939).

The characters, the story, the switch from sepia tone to brilliant color just as the plot was getting interesting, Dorothy's cute pigtails, blue gingham dress and shiny ruby slippers, Glinda's optimism and the Wizard's secret—all of it was magic. All of it was intriguing. But there is a part of the story that doesn't get a lot of attention. That is the tornado. Although that part of the movie doesn't last long, it is a critical part to the plot if you think about it. Everything changed in the story, especially for Dorothy, after the tornado.

Tornadoes are obviously scary weather phenomena that often result in damage to property and loss of lives, and that cause us to need to find a safe place in our homes if we even think one is in the area. In the midwestern United States, there are threats of them every spring and fall. However, this movie did not portray this particular Kansas tornado as all that scary. Dorothy did hit her head from the force of her house being tossed into the wind. But afterwards, she got up, looked out her window and found a fascinating scene outside her bedroom window.

What could have been a terrifying moment in the movie, is actually quite whimsical. Dorothy looks out in wonder as some of the people she knows actually float by her, almost untouched and going about their daily routines (in the air). Alternatively, she saw other people change before her very eyes in the storm, switching personalities in what most would consider pretty disturbing ways. But it is a movie intended for children, so again, it isn't that scary.

When it was over and the house landed on the Wicked Witch of the East, everything was definitely different. As Dorothy emerged from her battered farmhouse, bleary-eyed and adjusting to her new surroundings, she began to meet a variety of new people. Although they weren't speaking a different language, they might as well have been. Because it took a while for Dorothy to realize that they were looking for something from her that she never would have anticipated.

Everyone in this new land was looking to Dorothy for answers and leadership. Even though she was entirely new to this colorful and brilliant world that was just thrown into all kinds of chaos, they chose her to be the leader. Simply because she happened to be in the house that solved one problem that had plagued her new friends for some time, she quickly found out that she was supposed fix all kinds of problems for herself and these people, even though she had no idea what the solutions might be or how she and the others might figure them out.

Sometimes in real life people are thrust into leadership roles during crises. Whether one is chosen to lead because of the difficulties that have begun to plague an organization or it has dissolved into chaos soon after the leader is chosen, walking into chaos and crisis as a new leader can be the most challenging situation of one's career. It can cause one to question many things:

- What tools do I have to exist, let alone thrive and lead others through dramatically chaotic times?
- How can I prepare knowing that a new position will require these types of traits?

- What skills and strategies should I be practicing in order to bring about order and normalcy in an already complex organization?
- How can I learn these things even if I am in the midst of confronting chaos of the highest order?
- What do I do when I cannot seem to stay healthy and balanced while I'm supposed to be leading others and helping them to stay healthy, regulated and balanced?

Leaders seek out challenges and are chosen based on a set of skills they possess, their personalities, their experiences and their beliefs. From the employment application through a sometimes very lengthy search process, potential leaders are questioned, vetted, reviewed, Googled and reference checked until the entire representative group that has been charged to make this decision feels they have found the perfect or at least, best candidate for this position.

The candidate must not only be right because of her skillset, she must also have the right potential for any future work. She must have shown that she will be able to lead an organization not only now, but into new endeavors and new directions. If done well, the selection process should yield just the right person to lead at that given time in the organization's history.

Any new leadership role requires specific skills. Oftentimes, they are skills that all good leaders possess and utilize regularly. New leaders must practice these types of skills religiously. A new leader hired to maintain a history of excellence in her organization must do her research, reflect often, talk with others about how they are achieving their outcomes and continue to learn and adjust as she becomes part of her new home.

New leaders in this situation must take time to create authentic relationships, realizing that time is a critical ingredient to mutual trust. Conversations should be about listening, asking the right questions, hearing where an organization feels they are strong, where they might be able to grow and what opportunities there could be for quick wins. She should be picking the low hanging fruit and using it to cautiously and quietly begin to build on the existing structure of stability and success, grounded in new relationships, responsiveness, kindness and respect.

She should be systematically and personally connecting with all aspects of the organization. She should be looking for potential long-term goals and how they will align with current priorities and plans. This approach to new leadership is strong and will yield solid results in terms of a seamless transition. It requires skills and strategies, it requires time and it requires thought and planning.

Other times, new leaders are hired to determine a new direction for the organization. They are asked to facilitate a process of strategic planning where the organization revisits priorities and adjusts focus. In this type of leadership situation, perhaps the organization has slowly encountered change over time and new leadership is required in order to see the challenges with fresh eyes.

A new leader in this position can slowly introduce themselves, their thoughts and ideas and convey the reasons they were hired to all the stakeholders. Each group should have time with her through a systematic process. Thoughts and opinions should be solicited and shared. History can be discovered and explored. Sometimes it will get emotional, sometimes it will be full of data and evidence.

This process though, is a way for the new leader to start building her relationships and reputation in the organization in order to ultimately set a new or adjusted course. Time to do this is necessary and leads to a gradual increase in trust and team-building with a focus on change and often an exciting and much-needed new direction that folks can arrive at collaboratively and with a sense of collective ownership.

But what if the organization is looking for a leader in a time that is uncertain for them? What if the organization doesn't know who or what they are about anymore? What if the team chosen to interview and select the new leader doesn't actually understand the inner workings of the organization or what it needs? Or, what if after hiring their new leader, every single thing the organization had done in the past is no longer applicable to the future? How can anyone be the "right person" to lead at that point?

The following chapters will explore the ways that new leaders, especially inexperienced ones, can determine the state of a new organization (or any situation) which seems to be experiencing chaos and then outline ten strategies for a leader to utilize once she discovers that she has walked into chaos; once she discovers she is in the middle of the tornado and that she is charged with leading the journey of recovery and restoration. These strategies are intended to work together. Although it is difficult to maintain a focus on all ten of them all the time, that is the goal.

Leaders will make mistakes and will need to refocus on some of these strategies (or all of them) at some points throughout their journey. However, these ten strategies are critical for survival in times of great distress and will create the conditions for new teams to create a path forward. They will support the curation and nurturing of new relationships *through* the meaningful, but very difficult work of managing crises, instead of avoiding it.

Utilizing the metaphor of Dorothy and the Wizard of Oz (Fleming 1939) is intentionally meant to ground these strategies in a familiar story, to anchor a leader choosing to read this book in a world that is familiar. Leading in a new place that is filled with chaos, can feel like an unfamiliar and scary new world every single day. Each chapter is structured to present a strategy metaphorically tied to the story. There are practical implementation strategies presented in each chapter, as well as reflection questions to support the development of an action plan. Finally, each chapter presents questions for reflection and planning for the leader's self-management and self-care.

Self-care has become a more prominent topic of discussion among school leaders of late. Unfortunately, this is because many school administrators have been struggling with staying healthy and balanced during an unprecedented crisis and challenge. The truth is, leaders cannot support their employees if they are not mentally well themselves. It is not a luxury. Self-management and self-care are imperative. It is becoming a leadership norm, as it should. Take these suggestions seriously and don't wait until you can't lead and you are putting your responsibilities on others, before you address your own health and well-being. It is irresponsible and a sign of weakness to be tired and struggling all the time.

Although each strategy can stand on its own in strength and be a support to any leader, there is an order here to support moving from chaos toward normalcy, helping a new leader to gradually take one step at a time, if she chooses. For the experienced leader who is just looking for some ideas on how to manage crises personally and professionally, perhaps in a position that she is already familiar with, each of these chapters can be read in any order and will hopefully provide some new ideas or in the very least a reframing or new representation of old ideas.

After the tornado, after Dorothy makes new friends and leads them to find the truth about themselves and their new world, Dorothy's world finally gets back to normal. In this new normal though, she has gained insight about where she is from, those she loves and most importantly about herself.

She has learned about her strengths; she has learned that she can be resilient and resourceful. She has learned that she can be brave and lead even when she is intimidated and afraid, even when others think she can't. Even when others try to convince her and her new friends that she can't lead, every minute of every day.

After the tornado Dorothy is stronger, wiser, and ready for more challenges. She also has some great new shiny red shoes. Utilizing these strategies will hopefully result in some shiny new thoughts. They can become a foundational support for you and your new organization. Ultimately, leadership through chaos can help one become a stronger, brighter and more beautiful person inside and out. This type of leader can support the building and sustaining of an organization that feels like home to her and her colleagues. And we all know from this classic tale, there really is no place like home.

Chapter 1

Spot the Storm

"Unusual weather we're having, ain't it?"

—*The Cowardly Lion*

The first day as the leader in a new place can be scary, but it can also be very exciting. You immediately begin to meet new people, you start assessing your environment, and you begin planning. It's hard not to do these things. This new organization has placed its confidence in you. Whatever your specific responsibilities will be as a leader, you will certainly be focused on making a good first impression, asking a lot of questions and learning from those around you.

Any new place is going to feel different at first. You will see some of those differences readily and some of those differences won't show up for a while. If this isn't your first job, you will also be noticing similarities to your previous experiences. If you were hired to continue a tradition of excellence, you will be looking at this new place through that lens. Well-maintained systems and routines, a friendly atmosphere, productive conflict, would all be hallmarks of organizations that are functioning very well and your job will be to find your place in this new system and discover how you can make your mark someday.

If you were hired to create change, you will be looking through that lens. Noticing things that can be improved, asking questions about what people are proud of, making notes about what you are learning and what resources you will need in order to develop your vision. Relationship building will be a top priority and many people will be excited to meet you and get started in the work. Some will not, but they will find out eventually that you will be a leader interested in involving many people in your change process and the trust-building will begin in earnest from the very earliest conversations.

Whatever your understanding is of the reason you were chosen to lead, as you are acclimating to your new surroundings and beginning to make notes, you may begin to find yourself feeling uneasy because none of the interactions mentioned above are happening. You'll think at first that this feeling is just because you are not used to the culture, or that you're just nervous about proving yourself. You may even ignore the feeling for a while. You might keep it close to your chest and not share that you are feeling uneasy with anyone, or you might reach out to former trusted colleagues to pick their brains. Day after day, if that feeling continues to grow and become more intense, you might start to wonder what kind of place you have wandered into. Your intuition will be telling you that there is more here than just you being new. Listen to that feeling. You may be starting to sense chaos.

Oxford Dictionary (Dictionaries 2022) defines chaos as "complete disorder and confusion." It can be difficult to imagine that you would be hired for a new position without any knowledge of chaos and crisis and then find that everything is in complete disorder and confusion when you arrive, but it happens. With the online tools that we have now, access to information and news articles, if things were that bad, you would know that going in if you had taken a moment to research this place.

The truth is though, there can be chaos under the surface of a place that seems to be functioning well. So, how can a new leader quickly determine if what she is feeling is chaos? How can she recognize the signs of complete disorder and confusion? Aside from being faced with very obvious signs like a new technicolor reality filled with witches and a yellow brick road, or a global pandemic, there are some attributes that are consistently present in organizations in the midst of chaos—in the middle of a storm. There are many other characteristics, but these are some of the most impactful to the entire organization, and to the continuation of crises and dysfunction.

PERVASIVE GENERAL CONFUSION AND ANXIETY

It's normal that people will be anxious when a new leader comes into an organization. It takes time to build relationships and trust. Expectations are unknown, workflow may need to be adjusted day to day, and even big priorities may change. Most people will be ready you to set ambitious goals that may require more work from them and adjustments than some are not willing to make. Some will decide before you arrive, what they are willing to do and not willing to do. Many are planning for what they will do if they do not find your leadership to be compatible with their individual goals and priorities.

These are normal fears, anxieties and behaviors. With time and through purposeful conversations, many times new leaders and their employees can learn about each other and each other's goals in a nonthreatening and thoughtful way and come to mutual understandings and plans to move forward together as teammates. Leaders can foster that type of trust and mutual respect when the organization is functioning well, and there is some level of trust already established.

In chaotic organizations though, a new leader will encounter confusion and anxiety from the very start and at every turn. Because of this confusion, you will be forced into making decisions quickly, between the way things have been done in the past and the way she wants to do them in the future. Your interactions with individuals, sometimes your very first interactions will be filled with stress and uneasiness and a great deal of intensity. There will be a disregard for history and background from some. From others, there will be an overreliance on storytelling and background-providing as you seek information to make the decisions that are presented to you as emergencies. There will be a growing or immediate impatience if you are reluctant to decide things quickly, as well.

A chaotic organization and the members of it will not be ok with you stating that you would like to "see how the organization runs" before making any changes, because in truth, the organization is not able to "run" at that moment, without you making all the decisions. Individuals will become increasingly anxious each time they have to inform you that there is no policy, procedure or plan in place for something that needs to be accomplished and that they need help from you, this very new person. They will know that you don't know all the facts, but they cannot wait for you to learn. They will expect answers and quickly. They will expect you to lead and will be angry or scared when you do and when you don't.

Ultimately, every time a decision is made in order to keep the organization running, you will be confronted with people who are happy with the decision and people who are angry or confused, only adding to the general sense of anxiety and fear. Those who become anxious about these issues (which will more than likely be everyone at some point) will be talking with each other about how upset they are with all the new problems that are popping up because of what you've already "changed."

This is one reason there will never be a honeymoon period for a new leader of a chaotic organization. She will feel pressure building as she continues to make the decisions that are needed and as those decisions and their impacts, intensify the storm.

LACK OF DIRECTION

Many times in a well-functioning organization undergoing a change in leadership, the future direction of the organization is not changing. The leader is chosen to maintain the good work that has been accomplished and decision-making processes can be guided by a shared understanding of the direction everyone, or at least most people, feel the organization is headed. In this type of situation, the new leader needs to make it a priority to get up to speed on that vision and direction and really understand the history and reality of them before she does anything else.

At other times the new leader may need to determine a new direction, but that can be done through collaboration and communication. In a healthy, well-functioning organization employees can be guided by the existing vision, mission and strategic imperatives that have been agreed upon and are part of a collective set of beliefs and experiences. These shared understandings will not stop conversations from being difficult at times as the new leader explores opportunities to define that new course of action, but they will provide a solid foundation to have the discussions that need to be had in order to gain collective ownership and shared agency to move forward in a different direction.

The second cornerstone of chaos is that a new leader will quickly find that very few, if any individuals in your new organization can clearly articulate the purpose, direction, vision or mission, new or old. If you encounter confusion and anxiety as you seek information to make decisions, you will begin to take a step back from "how things have been done" to "where are we going or what are we about?" If these questions are also met with silence or head shaking from most, this is another clear sign of chaos.

Strategic plans may be in place but may have not been clearly articulated, or actualized. Or, there might not be a plan at all. You might also encounter people who think the previous direction was not good and are just "doing their own thing." Either way, the lack of direction and the realization that you are finding out about it, also adds to the confusion and anxiety of everyone involved as they anticipate your next steps.

LACK OF DOCUMENTATION/DOCUMENTATION THAT NO LONGER APPLIES

If conversations are yielding confusion over how things are supposed to be done and the new leader finds that individuals can't clearly identify where they have been or where they are going, you will surely begin to look for documentation that can help to shape your understanding of the current reality or to inform your decisions. Highly functioning organizations memorialize their processes and procedures to ensure continuity of operations and support for future decision-making.

If the documentation isn't there or if none of it applies to the current situation, that is another sure sign that the organization is in chaos or is at least going to have a difficult time operating for a while. It is true that handbooks, policies and procedure manuals aren't always referred to when they should be, but when they are needed and missing, they all of a sudden become critically important.

In the absence of formal documentation, many leaders will start to look for other sources of "documentation" like emails, memos, meeting agendas, and minutes. While these can be helpful, they are often not complete and at times even contradictory. They are often full of extraneous information and cannot be used to actually determine history, procedure, or process.

Additionally, since the leader is new, she will need to solicit help from people to find these things. Unfortunately, because everyone is already nervous, even asking some folks to help find things may quickly indicate who the leader values and who she doesn't just based on who is asked to help. That will not be any new leader's intention, but that is not important. Perception is reality.

Asking people to help you at this early stage may also indicate to some that you "don't know what you're doing." Why would she be asking for help from people, wasn't she hired to be the leader? Shouldn't she be helping us? At that point, this may become the narrative about you for some people. This type of story, which will definitely circulate, will muddy the already very muddy waters and further alienate you from your new colleagues and possibly your new community.

Sometimes you won't ask people for documentation but folks will bring it to you anyway, as a way to influence your perceptions and decisions. These "artifacts" may offer you a false sense of security that you are acting on good information. If you or the organization begin relying on items like these for "documentation" there will be a lot of time wasted on searching, discussing, and interpretation that just isn't necessary. This will set you back timewise, on gathering information that might actually prove helpful.

If you find that you are so desperate for information that you are down to looking for informal documentation like this, or if this kind of information is being presented to you in an unsolicited manner, it's important to stop looking for documentation at that point. Reading inaccurate documentation is like traveling down a rabbit hole (a different children's movie) and will not lead to any benefits at this time in the fact-finding process.

STORYTELLING

Taking a lack of documentation one step further, if no type of documentation can be found, oftentimes organizations in chaos will rely on storytelling to reconstruct the past or forecast the future. While storytelling will be discussed later as a strategy for building connection and demonstrating authenticity, when an organization is or has been in chaos, the early and oftentimes unsolicited stories make things more confusing. They can also be full of judgment and accusation. Stories will be used to illustrate things that went well or wrong and many times include personal opinions or anecdotes that aren't helpful to a new leader as you look to define existing issues or a path forward.

Any new leader in an organization in chaos, will try to connect to individuals and learn about them through conversation and personal interaction. But instead of learning about the individual, you will find yourself listening to the stories that individual wants to tell you to inform your perception of the organization and their place in it. The introductory stories may sound like a way for people to connect, but often do not provide you with the facts you need to make decisions or to lead through the uncertainty that everyone seems to be experiencing.

BLAMING AND SHAMING

Often the stories that people tell in this type of situation come with some information about others in the organization. Sometimes about coworkers of theirs, sometimes about other leaders in the organization or even your predecessors. It can be tempting to listen to these stories and think, "I would never do that!" or even to reassure the folks coming to you with the stories that you surely would never have done what they are accusing someone else of doing. As a new leader, it is normal to want to reassure people that they can trust you, and help them to start to learn about you, your values and how you like to lead.

Unfortunately, many times these stories are just that, stories. They do not convey the whole or complete truth. Listening is important to a point. Validating is tricky and not recommended, at all. These stories which can be full of blame, do little to foster trust and definitely do not create a solid foundation to build a new relationship. In fact, just the sharing of these stories can create foundational conditions for a relationship that is not healthy. Gossip is never a healthy relationship starter and if you engage in it, it won't be long before that becomes your reputation and your people begin to lose trust in you.

If you find yourself in the middle of a story about a terrible former leader or current colleague, it is wise to politely ask that the conversation be over at that point. Calmly let your new colleague know that leadership is really difficult and that you understand that many leaders have challenges and that you have had them yourself at times. If individuals in your new organization seek to create connections with new leaders in this way, the organization is probably functioning in chaos and the stories they are telling you (and others) are more than likely perpetuating that chaos.

SHUTDOWNS AND FEAR

In any organization, everyone approaches chaos differently. While some seek to share stories, others shy away from any interaction at all. They may shut down when a new leader approaches and asks for a conversation. They may be afraid based on past experiences to say anything, to validate anything or to share anything. Some individuals may be triggered easily by what you might think is a very benign question or conversation-starter. This combined with others actively seeking you out to share stories of blame can signify that there is a high level of chaos and distrust in your organization.

In an organization that has a strong culture, but is met with a crisis that threatens how everything is normally done, shutdowns and fear are also common. Working in a chaotic situation that is changing daily, requires that everyone in the organization not think too far into the future. Day to day survival becomes the norm and at times, this type of existence can lead folks to shut down or at the very least, lose a great deal of productivity.

Fear of what is happening or what is coming next often creates the conditions for emotional dysregulation, as well. In this situation, individuals seem to no longer exhibit the professionalism they can and have been able to in the past. This can often be scary for a new leader as well, as you will be consistently asked and even expected to keep your people "regulated," by managing their emotions for them through interactions or decision-making. In either case, individuals shutting down or exhibiting fear during regular conversations can be another sign of chaos and one that you should keep a close watch on.

DISTRUST

Ultimately, an organization displaying any, some or all of the above characteristics will more than likely be challenged with trusting you and each other. Whether it's due to the changing nature of their circumstances, or leadership and organizational challenges they have experienced in the past, it will be easy to see that the trust level is low between colleagues and their leaders. This may feel like it is personal, but this lack of trust may be just because of the position you hold.

The health of any organization depends on high levels of trust between colleagues and the leadership. In a chaotic environment displaying these characteristics, trust is a concept that is difficult for folks to even imagine. They themselves are looking for proof, just as you are, of what has happened, what is happening now and what will happen in the future. Individuals rely only on themselves in this circumstance and advocate only for themselves and their closest allies. This contributes to an even further diminished sense of trust and can lead to very unhealthy cultural norms, which can continue the cycles and patterns of chaos.

If any or all of these are present, it's worth noting that folks outside of the organization may not know about it. From the outside, stakeholders and partners in the work may see a very different picture. For this reason, it's important to talk with trusted colleagues who have worked with the organization or experts in your field in order to verify that what you are seeing internally is accurate.

But be careful in the conversations with previous leaders. Working in a chaotic place can cause one intense feelings of anger and frustration. Previous leaders may have left because of the stress and toxic culture you are now entering. Their experiences will be colored by what working in that organization did to them personally and professionally. Take all of their information, and everyone else's, with a grain of salt and realize that you are a different leader and you are working to create a different experience for you and your new colleagues.

Mentors, consultants and colleagues in the field can be invaluable and need not know specific names of your new colleagues in order to provide a sounding board and a third-party perspective. You can and should seek out anyone who is willing to listen and ask critical questions to help you reflect on what you are actually experiencing and to determine the current state of your organization, quickly. Determining this quickly is key, as strategies need to be put in place in short order so that you can set your own healthy boundaries, avoid as many landmines as possible and begin to stabilize the environment and set a path forward for everyone involved.

Don't forget that as you are recognizing and coming to terms with your new reality, you are also simultaneously bringing hope to those who want to be hopeful and who want to see a change. Before Dorothy came out of her house and realized that she had landed on the Wicked Witch, there was a sense of hopelessness in Oz. Even though there was a very long road ahead and no one knew if Dorothy really had what it would take to get them to the end of their journey, just her being there, being willing to listen, be a witness to the confusion and frustration and be willing to understand and take the first steps as a leader was encouraging for every one of her new friends.

New leaders realizing they have walked into a chaotic organization need to take stock of their own health and what they will need to do in order to stay strong for the road ahead. The strategies presented in the following chapters will be helpful, but knowing yourself is key. Family, friends, hobbies, meditation, healthy eating, and good sleep hygiene are all ways that a new leader can ensure they are strong enough to keep going, and leading a long road of recovery for the organization.

If after reading this chapter, you've identified that you're dealing with a chaotic new culture, it is time to begin creating a plan of action. Each chapter, beginning with this one will end with questions for you to think about as you start to document your journey and your plan. After that, there will be some questions for reflecting and planning for your own self-care and self-management. Again, this is not a negotiable aspect of leadership. If you neglect managing yourself and your emotions and thoughts as part of your work, the consequences to your own health and to the health of your close and personal relationships and your colleagues, could be great.

Finally, there are two sections at the end of each chapter outlining resources from the field of education as well as outside of education to learn more about the specific content outlined in each chapter.

REFLECTION QUESTIONS FOR YOUR ACTION PLAN

- How many and which of the characteristics listed above do you see in your current organization?
- Are there others who see them, as well?
- Who are those people and have you connected with them about your shared experiences and observations? Would that be helpful to you or not at this point?
- What evidence have you collected?
- What are the most impactful issues and why?
- How can you learn more about whether these issues are occurring, if you aren't sure?
- When can you build time into your calendar to begin creating your plan of action?

SELF-MANAGEMENT PLANNING AND REFLECTION

- What is the best way to let your loved ones know that you have determined that the state of your new home is not healthy and will need a lot of your time and attention?
- How will you reassure them that you will not forget your other roles in life, but that for a time, you will be facing some really big challenges that will take a lot of your time and energy?
- How can they support your journey by reminding you of what keeps you healthy and supporting you in those efforts?
- Will you be receptive if they do remind you? Be honest with yourself.
- How will they be able to hold you accountable for keeping those habits up?
- How can you let them know that you intend for everyone in your life to come through this journey intact and still strongly connected to each other?
- When can you build in time for personal reflection each day on your calendar?

A RESOURCE FROM THE FIELD

In his book, *The Challenge for School Leaders: A New Way of Thinking about Leadership* (Warwick 2014), Ronald Warwick, professor at Concordia University-Chicago, offers assessments for determining the effectiveness of your school's *instructional* program. If, as you are talking with your staff about the state of the organization, they indicate concerns that the instructional program of your school is lacking, you may be able to use the tools in this book to guide them through an audit as you simultaneously assess the aspects of culture discussed in this chapter.

Through "working on the work" you will be able to further assess cultural norms and tendencies in what most would consider relevant conversations. Then, you might be able to directly tie that information to the chaotic behaviors that you are seeing and documenting as potential issues that could help move your organization forward on the goal of improving instruction and ultimately student achievement and growth. Doing this may help to create a sense of urgency and may accelerate the pace of change for the cultural aspects that are troubling.

A RESOURCE FROM THE OUTFIELD

Many of the resources in this section will be podcasts. This is because your time is limited right now, and listening is something you can do while you are multitasking. Your commute, making dinner, folding laundry, going for a walk or working out are all times that you can be engaging in learning. The podcasts that I highlight here are all incredibly engaging and easy to listen to, as a bonus.

Adam Grant's *WorkLife Podcast* (Grant 2022) is a game changer for any leader looking for practical strategies to identify harmful habits, systems and behaviors in the workplace and strategies to improve them. It's easy to listen to, brief, and points to many other resources that can help a leader dig deeper into their organizational analysis and find support from experts in many different fields.

Chapter 2

Chase the Storm

"I've got a feeling I'm not in Kansas anymore."

—Dorothy

Once you have determined that you are currently in, or are going to be walking into a chaotic situation, it is critical that you learn what you need to in order to move the organization out of its current situation and forward on the path toward a meaningful and cohesive vision for the future. There could be any number of reasons that the organization landed in its current state and knowing all the reasons and the whole story is eventually important, but not as important as quickly determining the primary root causes and where you should focus your own new learning.

Trusting a new leader can be difficult for those who have been existing in a situation where they feel they alone are their only true advocate, or for those who suddenly find themselves on shaky ground after years of success and stability. A first step in gaining the trust of these folks is establishing yourself as a knowledgeable person, listener and someone who is genuinely interested in learning all she can about her new home and the issues it is facing. Actively seeking conversations and opportunities to ask questions is a top priority at this stage of your transition.

You will not be able to be an expert in all the aspects of leading a school or district on day one. That isn't possible for a new leader. Any CEO position is defined by a complex set of understandings, skills, strategies and relationships. However, even though *this position* is not your area of expertise, you were hired anyway. Rational people will not be expecting you to know everything there is to know about the Superintendency or the Principalship or if this is a new place but not a new position, you will not be expected to know everything about the organization. They knew they were getting a rookie and that's what they wanted.

If you find that there is no support from those who hired you or your superiors for taking some time to learn about the organization, and you find that they are hearing directly from your employees that you are not focused, not able to lead, etc., it is time at this point to review the aspects of the organization that you have observed already and let them know that you are concerned that there is cultural chaos and crisis that needs addressing.

Be blunt and provide evidence. Assure them that you are up to the task and that you will be providing them with regular updates. Ask them if they have seen these troubling behaviors and cultural norms. Listen to their concerns. Then, ensure that you have a commitment from them to come to *you directly* with their concerns. Ask them to shut down direct communication channels with your employees, at this point. If they are not willing to do these things, you may want to consider whether this is a place that you feel you can lead. You need the support of your superiors to do this difficult work.

If you feel you have this support, and are ready to move forward in digging deep and learning about this new place, you need to become knowledgeable in at least one area, and that is the situation that has thrown or is throwing your new organization into chaos. In the case of the COVID-19 pandemic, leaders needed to not only learn about the pandemic and related developments throughout the course of the virus, but how it would impact schools and ultimately children's ability to return to school. This issue would impact every single stakeholder in the community, neighboring districts and employers in the town.

In the case of other crises, like leadership turnover, unethical behavior, or any other issue, those will be the items that need your attention. These may be circumstances that are new to you and becoming an expert in what those unhealthy cultural issues can do to an organization, where the potential impacts are and how to move forward should quickly become your top priority.

UNDERSTANDING COMES FIRST

Not every organization in chaos is in the midst of a worldwide shared issue, like the COVID-19 pandemic. That issue was obvious. Sometimes, a new leader will determine the state of the organization through the red flags that were identified in the previous chapter after she has already begun her transition in. As she begins to ascertain that she is in a chaotic situation, finding out what the root issues are is critical so that the leader can begin her research into how to effectively move forward.

This may be obvious, but if you haven't already done an in-depth online search of your new workplace, now is the time to dive in and follow the leads. Look internally, as well, for historical news and publications, awards or articles in the archives. Put aside time to start to piece together the history from any documentation that you can find. Connect those dots with the red flags you are experiencing and create a timeline that includes big events and shifts in culture, climate or goals. Ensure that you have a clear picture of leadership changes, strategic shifts in priorities and changes in the bigger industry context which may or may not have impacted your organization.

Scheduling time to have strategic conversations at this point is also essential. Those who approach a new leader unsolicited with "information" or "insight" do not always have the intention of being unbiased and supportive helpers. As was discussed in the last chapter, often fear is running the organization and each individual feels a need to advocate for that which is important to them and their allies.

Have those spontaneous conversations and gather any information you can, but wait to draw any conclusions until you have met with a larger cross section of people from each part of the organization, internal and external stakeholders and even colleagues outside of the organization who have interacted on the fringes. Assume that in the first year, any information you are gathering from individuals or specific groups of people is incomplete.

Make it the goal of your conversations to hear what *has* been working, not just what hasn't been working, rumors or gossip. This forces your new colleagues to speak about areas they are proud of and things that they wish to continue. This may make some people uncomfortable, and that is important information, as well. Hearing what is working is a priority, though, because you might find yourself wanting to change things quickly in order to address the issues you are seeing on the surface or that others are bringing to your attention. If you don't know what is working (at least right now and at least for some people) and what is important to keep during your transition, you may cause more problems than you already have by making uniformed changes.

Ensure that you hear personally what is driving each person as they speak with you. Watch their body language and listen for what you can infer beyond what they are actually saying:

- Do they want to tell you about the organization or about why they are important to the organization?
- Are they only speaking to you because you asked?
- Do they want to find out about what your personal plans are for the future or what your history is?
- Are they interested in telling you about their colleagues' personalities or historical facts?
- Do they have thoughts about the future direction for everyone or just for themselves and their allies?

- Have they also tried to lead here and if so, how did that go?

The goal at this point is listening, asking the right follow up questions, taking copious notes and keeping your mouth shut outside of those conversations. Try not to formulate opinions about people through these initial conversations. These interactions are not giving you the most authentic information about people yet. Some people will have planned what they are going to say, some people might be very stressed just talking to you and others may not want to talk to you yet, at all.

At this point, it's also critical to ensure that you are not presenting any of the information you are gathering to anyone else, except your superiors. Keep that information at the highest level possible, to ensure that they stay out of the weeds. In this type of organization blame and storytelling may be present in all the stories that people come to you with. Even with your most trusted senior level team members, it will be difficult for them to hear what you are hearing from their colleagues and direct reports at such an early stage of your own relationships.

They might be the subject of the blame or they might be the saviors in the stories. You might be hearing about work histories, relationship issues and things that people have not disclosed to others before. Your senior leadership team will be dealing with their own issues of insecurity and trust and they will not know whether you can be trusted to sift through the information to find the whole and most honest picture of what is happening. Reporting any information back to them, while they are still learning about you and creating a relationship with you will not be helpful.

Remember that it is scary for a middle manager to know that his direct supervisor is listening to his direct reports and yet, you must. Encourage your senior team that your strategy at this point is simple, just gathering information and that you will be having conversations with them, too, in order to listen to their thoughts and perspectives. Let them know that your lack of disclosure to them is not an indication of your feelings or conclusions at this point and that you value their input, feedback and experience as the current leadership team.

During this time it is also incredibly important for you to be consistent in your approach to communication with everyone, and to do this it is important for you to maintain your own emotional stability. You may be hearing some very scary and controversial things about the people you are just getting to know. You may be encountering some big emotions and passionate feelings. Others may be projecting their feelings on you before you've even been able to learn their names.

Any fluctuation in your mood or approach to individuals will be noticed and talked about. Conjecture will be happening and fear increasing no matter your moods, but inconsistency will add fuel to the fire. People will be watching your facial expressions, your schedule, your office door and will be looking to find out who you've been talking with and what you are hearing. In the absence of your disclosure, there will be rumors.

Stay out of all of that for now and do your best to remain composed, positive about the future and consistently optimistic. You may find yourself questioning your decision to be a leader at this point, questioning your leadership team, questioning the future of this place, and all of that is normal, but don't share this with anyone in the organization. Reassure folks that you are here for the work and excited to learn and be a part of wonderful things that they have accomplished and what is coming in the future.

Here are some things to think about as you are listening and learning:

- Remain calm.
- Keep your journal and documentation with you at all times. The last thing you need is for anyone to find your notes and read for themselves the observations that you are making.
- Find yourself someone safe to confide in that is outside of your work life and personal life and who you trust to remain confidential.

LEARNING FOR THE FUTURE

Once you begin to draw some conclusions from the information you are gathering and can identify some of the reasons your new organization is in chaos, shift your research focus outside the organization to the issues that you feel need addressing which will have the most leverage for change. Unlike the old days of waiting for a movie to come on TV, you don't have to wait to get what you need, especially in terms of information and support.

Not only should you utilize existing resources, books, articles, and research papers, but you should and can utilize professional networks. Online chats and social media platforms can connect you to supportive groups of professionals that can be incredibly helpful once you have identified the issues you need to learn more about. Keep your questions broad, and focused on finding additional resources for you and your team.

The COVID-19 pandemic was an opportunity to collaborate with colleagues who were in similar situations, but very few colleagues in the field of education knew the specifics of the virus and its impact around the world on health and education. Reaching across to other fields of expertise became essential. Health care professionals, news outlets, and business podcasts were fantastic ways to learn new information and apply it in many different areas of planning.

Ultimately though, the importance is to learn, learn quickly and learn every day about the issue that the organization is facing. This is important because every conversation focuses in some way on the root issues of the chaos, whether they are obvious or not. While people may not say it explicitly, your interactions will eventually all reference the difficult areas because everyone is looking to you to figure out what the actual problems are, what to do and how to move forward.

If your conversations and internal research ultimately lead you to believe that the biggest issue that could lead to lasting change if it is addressed is a lack of systems for example, then your new learning should be focused on systems thinking. The issue could also be financial instability, unrealistic goals for the future or no strategic priorities. There are any number of reasons that your new organization is in this state, prioritize the issues and get researching.

AVOID RENOVATION

As you prioritize the issues you are seeing and settle on the issues you feel are most impactful, be careful that you are not choosing "cosmetic" issues as your top priorities. Educators and educational leaders like to have a lot of systems in place. There are a lot of forms, processes for processes, protocols, agendas, etc. Some of these can really impact what happens in the classroom with students, some of them just cause a lot of work that is very distant from instruction and that may never ultimately, truly impact the outcomes of a school or district.

If you are finding that some of these surface level systems aren't in place, that may be some of what is causing your chaos and crises. But, it also may be a symptom of deeper, cultural issues. Use your senior team to think through this. Perhaps curricular areas haven't been reviewed for some time and that is coming through as an issue for people. Present it to your leadership team and talk through what would happen to the current culture and climate issues that you are seeing, if that issue was to be addressed. Sometimes, there would be no real transformational impact at all, even though some folks would feel an item has been "checked off the list."

In fact, it may be true that initiating a fix for those kinds of issues could create some more chaos in itself if the underlying culture and climate issues are not addressed first. Undergoing a new and intense curriculum review cycle, for example, while there is little to no trust between individuals in the organization, may result in a feeling of relief at first, but may also create a great deal of busy work and more cultural difficulties.

Sometimes "working on the work" will create pathways for relationship improvements and there may be some individuals who think that addressing those issues will take care of culture and climate. Be cautious about engaging in that type of work too quickly before people have had the opportunity to weigh in on the potential impacts of that work, both positive and negative.

An organization dealing with toxic levels of chaos may have a lot of surface level issues or it may look as if everything is "in place." Dig as deep as you can to get to the root of the behaviors. Keep asking yourself, "Yes, that is an issue, but what caused that issue?" When you keep asking that question, you will be peeling the onion and may find that transformation will not come from surface level changes or tweaks. It is okay at this point for some of these types of issues to be ignored. Your priority issues, the ones that you should be spending your time learning about, may not have much to do with education, at all.

There are resources to address many of these issues. Some of them may come from other fields than your own. If there isn't research out there, reach out to colleagues in higher education who can help you identify a process to gather your own data with focused questions. Your mentors in the field are critical here. Others may not have experienced the level of dysfunction that you are, but they will most definitely have resources for you to begin reading so that you can become an expert at speaking about these issues within your organization. Resist the urge to throw your hands up in the air and resign yourself to just managing the chaos or to simply giving in to easy suggestions for improvement.

Remember, this new place of yours cannot operate in its current state. Your decision-making ability will be on display from minute one. Leaning back and watching the tornado swirl around you will not move you forward and will often increase anxiety and anger with those who are depending on you to lead. When folks come with stories, questions, decisions to be made, you must come to the table with knowledge as soon as you can. Arming yourself with knowledge will help you to keep calm and others around you calm.

Use every opportunity to let people know that you are researching the organization and that you have strategies at the ready. You will not be ready at the beginning with a long term plan and that is ok. But you have been hired as a leader and now more than ever, people need to see why. Leaders must be learners. They instill trust when they can be present, and just as importantly, present potential solutions. Take your time with this phase. Drawing the wrong conclusions or implementing the wrong solutions could drive you into deeper states of chaos. It may take a long time and you may go down a few different roads, so start this process of research and learning as soon as you know that your new home needs it.

As you identify potential issues and begin to research them, slowly begin to test the waters with your senior team:

- Have they noticed these patterns in behavior?
- Have they ever thought about what is causing the behaviors in the organization?
- What are their thoughts about the priority issues you have identified and how they influence their day-to-day operations?
- What have they already tried?
- Do they have any resources they are using now?
- What are their hopes and fears at this point?

Use the new information you are gathering to begin more fact-finding conversations, and to find out new and more specific information. Having these conversations builds trust on your team as they will see you taking steps to identify issues and potential solutions. Moving slowly enough and seeking their input before asking them to help you implement any changes or before forming conclusions about them and their organization, will also help everyone to stay as calm as possible through your transition.

As you engage in this process of listening, learning, discussing, listening some more, learning some more, etc., your conclusions might shift often and you might find yourself back at the drawing board, looking for a new path for your research and questions. Stay open and think like a scientist. Emotions are running high all around you, and the less you take it personally, the more successful you will be during this phase.

You have been identified as a leader for many reasons, and perhaps one of them is that you are a do-er. You may be a type A personality that relishes in accomplishing tasks on your list. Maybe you have successfully navigated transitions in the past, and you feel your method is tried and true, but it's not working here. You may be tempted to simply start. You may want to just *do something* to move everyone forward. Your colleagues may be pressuring you to do something. Your Superintendent or Board of Education may be doing the same. Let them know that you are learning and that what you are uncovering is going to require time to address. Stay calm, confident and focused.

Consider this step as a critical task to begin, but one that will not be done for a while. Be kind to yourself, as others may not be. There will be impatience, questioning about whether you are the "right person for the job" and whether you have a plan or not. Assure everyone that you do have a plan and that this is the first part of your plan.

Chasing storms is scary when you don't see the sunshine on the other side. Prediction is difficult if you are a new meteorologist. The swirling emotions, debris from failed initiatives, and haze and cloudiness of differing perspectives and histories will all serve to disorient you. Ground yourself in the knowledge that you are gaining about your new place, the priority issues and that the storm will eventually pass. You will have some calm moments, moments where you feel you have struck upon the climate patterns that led to this tumultuous time. Those may last or they may be fleeting, but gradually, as you listen and learn more and more, you will start to calm down and see the storm for what it is, just a weather pattern that will eventually clear up when the conditions improve.

REFLECTION QUESTIONS FOR YOUR ACTION PLAN

- Will addressing the issues you have identified as priorities, really be impactful for meaningful and transformational change?
- Are any of the issues that you've addressed simply going to cause more work but not have real impact?
- Have you been able to have casual conversations with your colleagues where you learn about their lives outside of work?
- Do you know anything about your colleagues' personal lives? Values? Commitments?
- Where can you strategically find time to keep having those conversations and building those relationships?

SELF-MANAGEMENT PLANNING AND REFLECTION

- Have you been able to build in time each day for personal reflection?
- Have you been strategic about scheduling opportunities for people (especially your leadership team) to give you feedback on your own process so far, not just what they are seeing in the organization?
- Are there people working with you who could support some of your research and fact-finding in order to free up some of your time?
- Is your physical environment at work supporting positive mental health for you?
- If not, how can you make your environment more comforting and supportive?

A RESOURCE FROM THE FIELD

In their book, *The Unlearning Leader: Leading for Tomorrow's Schools Today* (Polyak 2017), Michael Lubelfeld and Nick Polyak offer a new way of thinking about leadership. Inspiring leaders to think innovatively and "unlearn" traditional practices, Lubelfeld and Polyak give permission to all leaders to connect with other leaders, change practices that aren't leading to student growth and achievement and make a real impact, transforming their organizations for the better.

This book is about thinking outside of the box and realizing that you are never going to have the right answers. It is invaluable for any leader, especially a new one. In a chaotic environment, rethinking what you always thought worked, what your formal preparation told you would work, will be critical to your ability to bring vision and calm to your new organization.

A RESOURCE FROM THE OUTFIELD

In her podcast, *How's Work* (Perel 2019), international relationship expert Esther Perel utilizes her knowledge of interpersonal dynamics to engage personally with individuals working together and struggling through relationship issues that are ultimately impacting their success in the work environment. As you are digging in and learning more about the issues that your organization is currently dealing with, this podcast will offer helpful suggestions for how to coach as you are listening, gather more information and more importantly, help those in the organization to reflect on what they are actually experiencing.

Each of the podcasts is a one-time session with a pair of people that she will not see again. The conversations are real and very interesting to listen to. Esther is inclusive in her thoughts and opinions concerning relationships, gender identities and cultural norms and is an extraordinary resource for anyone looking to learn more about interpersonal dynamics and how we converse, problem solve and get along at work and in life.

CASE STUDY IN SPOTTING AND CHASING THE STORM: LEADERSHIP IN CONSTANT TRANSITION

Situation

A school district with a long history of high achievement and financial stability began to be unable to retain leaders. Through a series of leadership restructuring initiatives, the staff became increasingly siloed, and self-reliant. While many different "strategic plans" were written and developed in collaboration with the community, each new leader redefined the meaning behind the plans upon her arrival, and instituted her own set of new areas of focus. Often, because there was so much that needed attending to, each new leader instituted change quickly, creating not more stability, but more instability and distrust.

This constant turnover and lack of focus resulted in little to no trust from the staff in any new leader, no ability for them to focus on strategic plans, and instead a pervasive, districtwide focus on whether or how long the next new leader would stay and what changes would or would not take place before the leader inevitably left. After years of this type of leadership turnover, student achievement and growth were not a focus at all. The resources in the community, individual teacher commitment and each family's commitment to their own student's performance helped to shore up the inability of the district to remain focused on continuous improvement as a whole.

Staff morale was inconsistent, oftentimes reflecting not the successes of the organization in any traditional sense, but on the staff's ability to sustain through the new leaders, one after the other. The community was kind to new leaders, but often afraid that they would leave. However, that did little to support the work of new leaders trying to address the myriad issues left by each previous leader.

The district leadership team lost a key member and the Superintendent hired two new people to replace her. However, neither individual was prepped with regard to the actual issues that the organization were facing. The Superintendent was privy to some of the challenges, but not others, as he was focused mainly on operational functioning. The two new leaders were coming into their positions with experience in building and district leadership, however, in very different organizations. They quickly took note of the organizational challenges and began to feel overwhelmed at the difficulties that they were facing.

Overarching Challenge

To adjust the focus from inconsistent and ineffective leadership to effective instruction and ultimately sustained student achievement and higher levels of student growth in order to restore trust between the community, the teachers and the district office.

Cost of Not Finding a Solution

While student achievement remained high, student growth had stagnated and innovation and engagement (staff and student) were rare. The financial cost of continuing to turn over leadership was staggering. Professional development investments, time and energy bringing new leaders up-to-speed, time to build relationships with teachers, parents and students, time investigating the history and learning how the organization was or had functioned in the past, all led to a cost that was ultimately not moving the needle in terms of outcomes for students.

Additionally, each time a leader left, the culture of the community reinforced itself, and became more focused on the next leader, what they would or would not do and how to proactively prepare for that cycle to begin again. There was more time lost instructionally and more focused energy on adult actions and it became harder each time, for the new leader to effectively ascertain what was happening before she burnt out and looked for other opportunities.

Without addressing these issues, the district would continue to lose time, financial resources and trust from the community. Leaders would increasingly shy away from coming to work in this district. Students would continue to not be the focus of district efforts and would lose the opportunity to be challenged and engaged at high levels.

Solution

An intense focus on learning the entire history of the organization without personalizing the experience was needed in order to separate the intense anxiety, fear and frustration present from the reality of what the district had been experiencing. Focus groups, documentation, interviews with current and previous employees, and student and parent feedback were necessary to gain a complete understanding of what had been occurring prior to the new leaders' arrivals.

Research on organizational wellness and structure became the focus of their new learning, in addition to the practical mapping of the existing structures and culture. Underlying causes of instability and leadership team dysfunction were rooted out and brought to the attention of the current Superintendent and

Board of Education in order to address them head on. "Tweaking" of schedules, systems and processes was not effective. Instead, complete restructuring of staffing plans and responsibilities took place in order to realign resources and ensure that there was equity among all staff members.

The staff engaged in sustained opportunities to outline the many different initiatives they had been working on in the previous ten years, and worked with the administrators to find ways to build on all the experiences and professional learning they had been able to receive and determine what new learning they needed to do in order to address the current issues. Some teams required outside coaching to support their trust-building and development.

Trust building was slow with the new administrators, and ultimately the last piece of the puzzle to be put in place, but taking time to learn about the organization, not reinforce existing thoughts about leaders and leadership in general and ultimately bringing the cultural aspects of the district that were impeding continuous improvement and innovation into the light and focusing on moving forward with a commitment to improving those things eventually began to stem the tide of leadership turnover.

Dedicated leaders at all levels committed themselves to staying aligned and supportive of each other at the leadership level, no matter what, and this is what kept the chaos at bay, while moving forward on the goal of focused attention on instruction and students.

Chapter 3

Provide an Accurate Forecast

"Come along Dorothy, you don't want any of *those* apples."

—*Scarecrow*

Turning on the lights in the middle of the night is not an easy thing to do. No one wants to do it. It hurts your eyes, it reveals what you look like when you've been sleeping and it takes a while to adjust. Even the person who knows it's coming, who actually turns on the light, can feel the effects of the bright light on eyes used to the darkness.

When Dorothy woke up from being hit on her head during the tornado, she walked out from her sepia-toned farmhouse to the bright light of Oz. The colors were different, the light was bright and she knew very quickly she wasn't in Kansas anymore. She didn't have the benefit of camouflage and definitely could not hide from the folks just waiting to see who would emerge from the house that fell on them, literally.

Being new to an organization and practicing honesty about what you are seeing can feel just like this for the folks you are starting to get to know. Even if you know that the light is needed so that you can begin to solve the problems ahead, it is still scary to turn it on. You don't know how it will be received, and it hurts those who have been existing with the lights off. Chaos can only exist in darkness. Bright light creates vulnerability, but eliminates hiding places and reveals issues that were easily masked in the dark.

So far, you've been a tremendous listener, a great notetaker and questioner. You have done your research, come back with questions, researched some more and hopefully with your leadership team, you are now feeling fairly confident that you have drawn some accurate and helpful conclusions about the state of your new organization and the root causes of the storm that is raging around you and your new colleagues.

Hopefully, through the steps you've already taken, you have had many opportunities to cultivate the beginnings of trust and relationships, especially on your senior leadership team. Your stable and consistent demeanor has hopefully led folks to feel confident that you are not going to overreact or problem solve impulsively. You haven't changed anything that matters to people and that is working for the organization and haven't created more problems through those types of actions.

So far, you have gently and quietly moved through the storm taking the temperature, monitoring the shifting winds and predicting the storm's next moves to the best of your ability. Some people might be calming down and some might be getting more anxious. If your listening and calm demeanor was needed by some, they will be feeling that they are in good hands. For those who have been missing and wanting a leader with hard and fast answers, they might be even more anxious than when you arrived. For those feeling protected by the darkness and chaos, they may be getting angry that you have been digging to find out what is actually going on.

Either way, your budding relationships are about to be hit again by the storm that continues to swirl. But this time, you will be the primary source of the discomfort. You might be about to become the storm. You are about to start telling the truth about what you have learned on your storm-chasing, fact-finding mission through the tornado. Some people will be prepared for this as they are aware that you have been listening and learning. Some people have been actively avoiding you and hoping you would just go away. They will not want to hear what you have to say.

You have communicated that you were doing all this work so that you could develop the right plan to move forward. Some folks will not be ready for it. No matter how much time you've taken, some folks will never be ready to actually hear and listen to what you have to say. They may be afraid of what will be exposed, or they may be afraid of the work it will take to move forward. It doesn't matter. Stepping out from the storm into the light is intense for everyone involved, but a necessary step.

COLLABORATE ON YOUR CONCLUSIONS

As you begin to prepare how you will share your observations and conclusions, ground your thoughts in research and evidence from the resources you have been reading and listening to, and also what you've learned about your new place from the individuals who have been there. However, avoid calling out people and departments specifically. Cite books and authors that have helped you work through the main issues with practical advice. Think about themes that are related to each other, and what groups in the organization those themes affect. At this point as you are preparing, you should be working with your senior leadership team.

Brainstorming sessions with them and focused discussions about what the most pressing issues are is important. Set your norms around these conversations collaboratively. Ensure that unless you need them to talk about this with anyone else, they are not to be sharing your conclusions or plans prior to when you are ready. If you cannot trust that to happen, then you will need to address that first with the individuals who are not living up to those expectations.

As you and your team discuss your thoughts, ensure that there are ample opportunities for them to ask you questions and provide more information to you. Ultimately, take ownership of these thoughts as your own, though. You're new here and this is your work as their leader. You will need to remain respectful and you make your observations and keep your tone curious. Be open to the feedback you receive as you are developing your presentations. But don't stray from being as honest as you can about what you are seeing and how you have learned that it is impacting the overall success of the organization.

Consider at this point, creating a secondary leadership team that is made up of formal and informal staff leaders, as well. Union representation, teachers, paraprofessionals, parents and even students can all be helpful to you in this process. You have been talking with your people and you should know by now who are the people that are most important to your work. They will be the people who are the most influential (positively or negatively). It is important to have them in this secondary group and to think through the information you are about to share with everyone and engage them in how to most effectively communicate it.

Build in time strategically with both groups to reflect on what you are going to be sharing and for them to give input. Prepare to have someone on your team (not you) taking notes as you facilitate these sessions. You may even consider recording these sessions so that you can look back at body language and other indicators of how the information is being received as it is being presented.

Pick appropriate times together to begin sharing your work with the bigger group and think strategically about how to share. Pick times that are less stressful and give plenty of notice through advance agendas and even carefully chosen reading material before your meetings. Prepare your presentations ahead of time. Practice and role play the actual presentations and questions that may come up and what your responses will be.

PURPOSE FIRST

Carefully organizing your observations and your plan for rolling out this new information is a critical step. Recognizing that not all of it needs to surface at the same time, is imperative. Begin with your purpose. Why are you here? What are you going to be working on in the coming months and years now that you have been able to learn more about this new place? This is not about mission and vision, because the organization may not have one. This step is to help the rest of the organization see the big ideas that you have determined are contributing the most to the chaos you are all experiencing.

You will want to keep these big ideas in the ether moving forward from the moment you share. There should be reminders of this purpose in each of your meetings, they may be posted on the walls, and certainly communicated in every conversation in which they are relevant. These big ideas and your purpose are going to guide your work going forward and should serve as an anchor for future action steps in your plan.

POSITIVES SECOND

At its very core, no matter what you have discovered, the purpose of your work together is continuous improvement. There *are* some good things happening in the organization, regardless of how difficult things seem right now or have seemed for a while. If you don't take time to recognize those things and call them out before you begin the hard work, you will regret it.

Trust levels are low when you begin to share your observations. If you neglect to include positives as you are sharing issues impacting the organization, you will risk your new colleagues not trusting your conclusions because you haven't taken the time to see the "whole picture," or more importantly, them as individuals. But, if you take time to honor the good things that they have accomplished in the past, the aspects of the culture that are healthy and supportive, anything really that is not toxic and contributing to the chaos, you will start to paint your picture in a familiar way.

Honoring the history of any organization is important, especially one who is experiencing chaos due to leadership turnover. Each leader may have come in with her own plan and the recent past may feel like the movie *Groundhog Day*. When you consistently, throughout your work in the years ahead, remember to admire what is working and going well, and what in the organization's history that folks can be proud of, people will learn that you are not here with any hidden agendas, but to help and move everyone forward and not start from scratch.

TRUTH THIRD

Start with sharing the truths that are most universally accepted. These may be historical facts and timelines or shifts, or they may be things that almost everyone is struggling with. But, by starting with some things that most people can agree on, you will be inviting most people to come *with* you on the journey and work toward solutions.

Move on from there to the new discoveries you've made that may be more difficult for people to hear. This is not about making a "positive sandwich" where you are giving great feedback and then putting the negative feedback before another reminder of how great the organization is. Instead, this is about organizing what most can agree on first and moving to those things that are not as universally accepted. These are the areas where there is division, discomfort and which if addressed, may be able move you the furthest forward.

Choose your words intentionally and script this out. It is very important that during this section, the revelations are carefully constructed to focus on particular issues and not on people. Make sure that individuals' comments or behaviors cannot be identified, but that you are instead making sure you present a laser-like focus on the most pressing issues, how they are leading to problematic aspects of the climate and culture, and how these issues are ultimately impacting, the effectiveness of the entire organization, especially in terms of outcomes for students.

The research you have done on these issues is important to utilize here, as well. You have spent a lot of time looking into why these issues are important to address, how to address them and why it will make a difference to everyone's satisfaction and engagement in the workplace. Incorporate those things that you have learned throughout this part of your sharing, so that everyone can recognize that there is validity to the concerns you are raising and that none of this is personal.

ACTION FOURTH

After you have revealed your purpose, positives and the realities that are creating this chaotic environment, talk through some of your immediate next steps. This is not about long-term planning. In fact, it should be emphasized that there will need to be a collective effort moving forward to plan to address the issues.

Reiterate often that you will come together to evaluate progress, make revisions, and start that process all over again as your continuous improvement cycle. Although there may not be many known next steps, omitting them at all will leave everyone wondering what you intend to do about what you have just told them is causing chaos in their organization.

END WITH HOPE, OPTIMISM AND REALISM

Finally, don't forget to end with hope. In an article for The Conversation (Worthington 2020), psychologist Everett Worthington explains that "hope is not Pollyannaish optimism—the assumption that a positive outcome is inevitable. Instead, hope is a motivation to persevere toward a goal or end state, even if we're skeptical that a positive outcome is likely." The information that you have just shared in one (or many meetings that are to come) will leave some folks feeling that there is so much work to do, that nothing may ever change. Additionally, they may have been through this before, where a new leader comes in and tries to tell them everything will be ok.

Leading with hope means that you are not telling them that everything will definitely be ok. It means that you are telling them it might be if you can work together as a group with a collective vision for the future. You have to convey a belief that your work together will make a difference and that ultimately, everything you are going to do, you are going to do together, and that it should make the organization better for everyone, especially for students.

You will not be able to create a culture on your own that is hopeful and optimistic, but setting the tone and helping people to see that they have the tools to make a difference, is one of the first steps. Remind them here, too, that even if they don't have the tools, you will be here to support them in learning what they need to learn.

LIVING IN THE LIGHT

Telling truths like this is like sounding the tornado alarm after a storm has already been quietly raging for days, weeks or even years. When you turn on the lights and sound this alarm, some folks might scatter and look for a way out. Some might feel relieved. Some will be surprised. Not everything that you are seeing is something that everyone else has seen. The goal during this process is not for anyone to validate your conclusions. They are just that, your conclusions based on the information that you have gathered and the goal is just for everyone to hear them.

More issues may come to light when people feel that the organization has been opened up. More people may come forward with stories. The listening and fact-finding and research will continue as the organization moves toward healing and further into the future. It's ok to go back and forth between these first two strategies to ensure that you are continuing your learning, your research and forward progress. Repeating this process ensures you stay on solid ground because you are continuing to keep the lines of communication open and your planning will continue to evolve.

Each time you present an issue and discuss it, ensure that you are providing background, context, positives, next steps and hope. Just putting an issue out on the table does not help if there is no optimistic or realistic path forward. Doing that only intensifies shame, embarrassment and anxiety or will provoke arguments between you and your colleagues or amongst colleagues in the organization.

Ultimately, your goal is to offer everyone a glimpse into what a leader sees. In a healthy and well-functioning organization that is not always necessary. Everyone may already know their role and appreciates that each has their own perspective. People trust that everyone else is doing their part and that when looked at in totality, the operation is healthy and that is why it achieves its desired outcomes. Leaders are privy to the different perspectives and offer coaching and support to match everyone's different needs, but not everyone needs to see all of that.

In a chaotic place, people have probably strayed out of their lanes to see what others are doing. They may be obsessing over ensuring that others are doing their part or they may be doing this to avoid the work that exists for them in their own lane. They might be doing this because they don't agree with what they should be doing, don't know what they should be doing, or aren't fully prepared to do what they should be doing.

Perspectives get very skewed when this occurs. Lines are blurred as departments or individuals attempt to address issues that are impacting them but are not being resolved in healthy ways. They may feel they are doing their level best to ensure that the place is staying afloat, but they are simply creating more complexity and confusion for everyone.

They cannot see that though, because only the leadership has the view of the entire landscape. Telling truths about what you see from your perspective is important to illustrate how chaos has affected and is continuing to affect every part of the organization and that a systematic, focused and collaborative response is needed in order to move forward together and achieve the goals that you all wish to achieve.

Dorothy remained curious and open-minded as she learned about Oz. The people were different from her, their fears were different from hers, they had a whole history that she wasn't a part of, but all of a sudden, she needed to find a way to help them (and her) achieve some collective and individual goals. She remained curious and nonjudgmental as she learned about them. She was kind in her observations (most of the time) and respectful that she was in a world that wasn't her own and that ultimately in order for everyone to achieve the desired outcomes, they needed to work together.

This step can be a very challenging aspect for a new leader. Staying calm, patient, and kind as you speak with honesty and confront the uncomfortable feelings and emotions of your new colleagues is imperative and can be very difficult, but it can be done, and it will move everyone forward.

REFLECTION QUESTIONS FOR YOUR ACTION PLAN

- Are you getting closer to a collective and coherent working knowledge of the current reality of your organization?
- Do you need to take any steps backwards so that you can understand the context better?
- Have any behaviors in the organization changed as you have begun to share your findings?
- Who are your current allies in the work?
- Have your allies shifted since you arrived?
- Where are your biggest obstacles and how might you be able to lean into those obstacles in order to diminish their impact?
- Have you been reporting your findings regularly to those to whom you are accountable?

SELF-MANAGEMENT REFLECTIONS AND PLANNING

- How is your mindset?
- Are you feeling personally attacked or have you been able to separate the attacks from you as a person?
- Are the thoughts and stories in your own head supporting you or tearing you apart?
- How can you remind yourself more often of your purpose and values, or ask others to remind you?
- Are you finding time to move your body during the day and eat healthy foods?
- Are you getting enough sleep?

A RESOURCE FROM THE FIELD

In his book, *What If I'm Wrong?* and *Other Key Questions for Decisive School Leadership* (Rodberg 2020), Simon Rodberg, a leadership coach and former principal, offers school leaders strategies for avoiding making quick decisions and rushing to judgment. As you are working your way through chaos and beginning to share the truth of what you are seeing, this book may support you with difficult conversations and decision-making protocols that can help you slow down and ensure that you are confident in the choices you are making.

RESOURCES FROM THE OUTFIELD

Brené Brown has been billed as many things, however in this author's mind, she is in the category of professor, researcher, general impact-maker. Her work changes lives, organizations and outcomes. In her podcast, Dare to Lead, (Brown 2020) she offers not only her own research and findings from working with leaders and organizations all around the world, she also gifts her listeners with conversations that highlight some of the most prominent leadership experts in the field right now and the most current leadership research.

She reflects regularly on how she and other leaders in her own organization apply her research and this is offered to listeners in an incredibly relatable and generous framework. The podcast consistently points listeners to other resources to learn more about how to handle specific leadership issues and each episode is packed with strategies and practical ideas for leaders in any field.

Chapter 4

Bring Everyone Along on the Yellow Brick Road

"We have nothing to fear, as long as we believe."

—*The Wizard of Oz*

As you're walking down this yellow brick road of gathering information, communicating your truth, asking more questions, and confronting realities with truth and honesty, it can be very tempting to keep these interactions as small and intimate as possible. You may be thinking that the information you are gathering and sharing should be on a "need to know" basis.

You have begun a process of sharing a lot of information and you know that trust is still low. However, the more these conversations and presentations are kept behind closed doors, only for specific audiences, the more rumors will likely be circulating about them. The antidote to that is to "open up" your conversations and invite more people to see and hear them. The idea of having these tough conversations open to many stakeholders to watch or listen to can definitely be scary. Some of the questions you might be having about this approach are:

- What if I make a mistake or say something I shouldn't when everyone is watching or listening?
- What if someone else shares something that is inaccurate in public and I don't handle it well or know what to say?
- What if others get upset with what they hear after the fact and don't talk with me about it?

These are all valid concerns. But here are some things to think about when considering whether you feel comfortable making your process or meetings as public as possible:

- Are you telling the truth?
- Is what you are sharing appropriate to share?
- In your narrative, are you avoiding blame and focusing on data and facts instead?
- Are you prepared to be vulnerable when you are asked a question you aren't prepared to answer in your meetings?
- Are you ready to have conversations with folks who disagree with you, and really listen to their concerns?
- Do you want your process to be accessible so that you aren't spending your time explaining what you're doing instead of doing the work?

If you can answer yes to those questions, then I suggest you are ready to make your conversations and presentations public and available. If your answer is no to any of them, then you may want to continue working on the first couple of strategies for a little while longer.

As you learn and engage in the feedback loop internally, continue to build trust with your colleagues and refine your conclusions, you will eventually feel prepared enough to have these conversations be more public because your confidence will have increased due to your knowledge of the issues. But why is it important to make your conversations public? Transparency is important, but why can't notes just be shared after meetings? Why do the actual conversations have to be public?

MISINFORMATION

Let's begin with transparency. A 2013 study (TINYpulse 2013) found that, management transparency is the top factor when determining employee happiness and satisfaction. The results were so unexpected that the survey summary noted, "This finding surprised us too, with management transparency coming in at an extremely high correlation coefficient of .937 with employee happiness. The cost of improving transparency is almost zero, but requires an ongoing dialogue between management and staff. We see an increasing number of companies using transparency to attract and retain top talent."

Rumors about tough conversations cause circulation of misinformation and that only heightens anxiety when there is no way for people to find out the "truth." It's like playing a game of telephone. Those people who are officially on the committee or in the meeting, attend the meeting where they hear what is going on directly from you. They interpret it the way they interpret it.

Those invited and involved in the discussions hear the questions and your answers, and they watch and interpret everyone's body language. Even if you give them specific notes on what to disseminate to others, they will put their own spin, thoughts, opinions, body language into their retelling of the meeting. That is impossible to avoid.

If you can allow anyone who may be interested or impacted by your work to just watch and judge for themselves, you won't avoid personal interpretation, but you may avoid spin. Creating an opportunity for folks to judge for themselves can be freeing. People who are interested will feel that you are letting them into your process and that will increase their sense of trust. You also will not need to spend as much time crafting your communication out to others after the meetings, as they have been offered the opportunity to be a part of it firsthand.

Inviting people in also increases accountability. No longer can anyone officially invited to the conversation just sit on the sidelines and rely on someone else to participate and make decisions and then blame them later. Or, those who aren't officially involved in the conversations cannot avoid the hard work because they were "not aware" of what was happening. At any point, they are welcome to join the process and catch up to where everyone else is.

Misinformation stemming from "trickle out" communication can be dangerous in a chaotic environment and it often leads to more work and more energy than you have right now. You are trying to get people to a common understanding quickly and efficiently. You do not have the time to correct people's perceptions of how something was said, whether something was said or what the tone of the meeting was. If folks have the ability to watch your process (preferably through recorded meetings) then when they hear rumors, they have the ability to "check the tape" themselves.

TRANSPARENCY IN COMMUNICATION

You have taken on this role of leader in a place that desperately needs you. Whether they knew it when they hired you or found out later, they know now that they need you to see them through this journey. Confidence in yourself at this point is necessary and non-negotiable. When you choose to make your process public, it demonstrates confidence in yourself and your team. But make no mistake, you are also making your leadership vulnerable. That is not a bad thing.

The act of bravery that it takes to invite everyone in, is enough to begin to connect you with those who are wary of you and who are afraid of change. You will be demonstrating that you intend to involve everyone who is interested in working with you, into your process. This courage will also continue to inspire folks who are ready for change to champion your efforts. If you can carefully plan your talking points and ensure you are confident with what you are sharing, and sharing it publicly, here are the benefits you will find:

- Increased sense of trust between you and your stakeholders
- Increased awareness of the issues you are facing and your plans to move forward
- More allies in your change process
- A common set of resources for people to refer back to if they have questions or concerns about your plan
- Increased sense of confidence in your senior team to be transparent with others
- Collective ownership

Remember that communication involves more than talking. When you make your meetings public, you may be tempted to always fill the time yourself. That is not necessary and in fact, can be detrimental. Create space in your meetings for folks to think and be silent, reflect, talk to others, ask their questions and discuss. Not everyone will be comfortable with this at first, but as you move through the process and engage in these types of meetings more often, people will become more comfortable and it will slowly become the norm. You need to listen in these meetings just as much as you need to speak.

THE PITFALLS OF TRANSPARENCY

When you decide to make your process public, there will be some downsides, but not many. Those who are unhappy with you may try to use your records against you. Be ready for those conversations by consistently reminding folks that your purpose is to support everyone's understanding of where you are in the history of the organization. You are expecting that there will be times when this process is uncomfortable, when people will make mistakes, when things will need to be clarified. But, assure them that you will always be honest. And if you cannot give them answers they are requesting publicly, you will tell them why you cannot. Obviously, protected personal information, health information, etc., cannot be shared publicly, but you wouldn't do that even in a meeting that wasn't being recorded.

Having most of your meetings in public will benefit you tremendously in this chaotic place. However, it does not replace the idea that your door should be open for anyone to talk with you privately about concerns as you move through your process and that you respect confidentiality when people share with you. Public meetings will actually invite more private and personal conversations, because more people will have the opportunity to share their opinions on what you are learning and going to be doing. The combination of these shared experiences, with increased opportunities for personal connection, will lead to collective responsibility and trust quicker than keeping your process private.

REFLECTION QUESTIONS FOR YOUR ACTION PLAN

- Do you have a well-articulated system for ensuring that you are communicating opportunities for everyone to participate in viewing your process when they can?
- Are there barriers inherently built into the system that don't allow people to participate? Schedules, workloads, relationship issues?
- If there are barriers, how can you address those issues at this point so that the opportunities to engage don't seem like empty promises?
- How do you specifically seek feedback on how you have been seeking feedback?

SELF-MANAGEMENT REFLECTIONS AND PLANNING

- Do you have someone to talk to yet outside of the organization that can help you process your feelings and emotions? If not, find someone now.
- Are you still approaching this work with a growth mindset and learning from the folks who are engaging with you, even when you are in public settings?
- Are you keeping up with your reflections and journaling?
- Are you still making time for your own health and well-being?
- How are your personal relationships holding up?

If this is becoming difficult, take some time to find out what your loved ones need from you and how you can find resources that will support your family unit during this time. This will require pointed and direct conversations so that you can come up with a plan together, and hold each other accountable.

A RESOURCE FROM THE FIELD

The National School Public Relations Association (NSPRA n.d.) is a resource to any school leader looking for support in communicating with all of her stakeholders. There is a wealth of expertise, available tools, and resources offered by this organization that can help not only in crisis communication, but also in evaluating the current communication and engagement planning of any school organization. If you are looking to increase opportunities for transparency and engagement, this organization can support you in a myriad of ways.

RESOURCES FROM THE OUTFIELD

In their podcast, *For Immediate Release* (Hobson 2022), Neville Hobson and Shel Holtz take a look at issues happening currently in the public relations arena. Although the issues are not directly related to the field of education, listening to the insights and learning provided by specific examples, can be helpful in managing communication from a proactive perspective and also support reactive communication management when necessary.

CASE STUDY IN PROVIDING AN ACCURATE FORECAST AND BRINGING EVERYONE ALONG: TRANSPARENT AND CREATIVE COMMUNITY COLLABORATION

Situation

A first-year superintendent began her tenure with her new district in the fall of 2020. She arrived with one month to help her new team determine how to open school for the first full year of the COVID pandemic. She had built no relationships, had no context in terms of community values or beliefs and the majority of her administrative team was new to their positions. Collaborating with her colleagues in the area, she found that many districts were planning on beginning the year with remote instruction however, this had not been effective in her current district, based on what she was hearing from her new Board of Education and what had emerged from their survey of the community after the spring lockdown.

Overarching Challenge

- To create a plan for opening school that allowed as many students in-person instruction as possible and provided students with remote instruction who wanted it while adhering to the health guidance and supporting her new team in their new roles so that all aspects of the plan were executed well.
- To avoid misinformation and ensure that all stakeholders understood why decisions were being made and how they would impact the school experience.

Cost of Not Finding a Solution

The new leader spent a lot of time listening in the first days of her transition to ensure that she had an accurate picture of how people were feeling about coming back to school. The community was already divided at this point in the pandemic, in terms of beliefs about the virus and solutions for school. She knew that in-person instruction was best for students, however, not all parents felt comfortable with children being in the building. Additionally, many staff were feeling uncomfortable with being back for health reasons, and others were worried because they would have child care issues if their own child's district stayed remote.

Staying remote for all children would be inadequate for the students in the district, but bringing teachers and staff back into school would be a cause of stress for teachers and might cause increased costs due to bargaining impacts of these decisions with the local collective bargaining unit. Preparing buildings for in-person instruction at that time required:

- Reallocation of room spaces to account for isolation rooms and spacing of students
- New and different types of furniture to ensure that students could be spaced out
- Signage and distancing reminders throughout all facilities
- New cleaning and disinfection protocols
- New screening protocols for symptoms
- Sanitation stations for students
- Adjustments to physical aspects of the buildings, like locks on water fountains
- Scheduling adjustments to account for teacher plan time in the event that teachers needed to cover for each other during the day if too many were ill or needed to stay home with their own child

She needed to find a solution that would account for as many family and staff member preferences as possible in order to reduce stress and anxiety and keep the focus on learning or the poor results of the remote learning experience from the spring of 2020 would continue. She also needed to ensure that as many people as possible understood why decisions were being made in order to keep anxiety at bay and avoid having to have many conversations with individuals on the same issues. There was just not enough time for that level of support and explanation.

If she couldn't address these issues, the cost to her team would be great in terms of the level of work to keep student achievement on track remotely, and the stress of supporting community members who couldn't support their children at home. In terms of community trust of her and her future in the district, these were on the line as she was so new and following a leader who was well respected and trusted for years.

Solution

The only solution to this situation was found in collaborating with her new administrative team, teachers and community, all at once. A task force was created with parents, Board members, community members and staff members to build the plan for the fall and each weekly meeting was broadcast online, recorded and kept online for anyone in the community to see. This process, while daunting at first, was a great way to avoid anxiety, rumors and misinformation and ensure that the process was collaborative.

The entire team collaborated early and often to determine exactly what they felt they had to accomplish together. Once they determined that there were only a certain number of students they could have in the buildings, the administrative team set out to devise a plan that would accommodate both students in the building and at home. The plan was unique at that time, and offered the remote platform to students at home and at school, ensuring equity for both groups in terms of instruction. This made parents who felt nervous about their students being in the building, more comfortable keeping them home because they were not trading a better instructional experience, for a safe one. It also allowed the district to utilize less substitute teachers, already at a premium, as teachers and staff could still teach students in the building remotely from their home if they needed to quarantine themselves or be home with their own children. The plan was presented to the task force regularly as the logistics were ironed out and all questions were addressed in this transparent format.

Every time they met they revisited their purpose and built off of what they knew they could accomplish. The team never shied away from presenting the truth of their situation, which was that there was no way to ensure that everyone would have exactly what they wanted, but they would get as close as they could get to that goal. Each meeting ended with action steps to be accomplished next and a collective recognition that the team could get through this together.

Ultimately, through this work and pushing through the chaos and difficulty, a very creative solution to educating students in a pandemic was borne. The district would utilize a remote platform for students that were both in the building and those at home. The community was asked to keep their students home if they could support them, but if not, the district would bring them in. Because there was equity in the platform, fully half of the community elected to keep their children home in order to ensure enough spaces for the students who needed to be in school to be there.

The collective bargaining unit worked together to prioritize staff medical needs or family concerns and organize staffing decisions around those issues. Staff accommodations were made through reorganizing class lists, class spaces and ensuring technology and personal protective needs were addressed. Trust between teams was built through these areas of collaboration, and the community came to trust the district as well, as the plan accounted for the varying opinions and levels of comfort in the community. It was very difficult work, but this process of ensuring that the work was collaborative, always based in the reality of the challenges and as transparent as possible, yielded great results.

Chapter 5

Wear Your Ruby Slippers with Pride

"Are you a good witch, or a bad witch?"

—*Glinda*

Dorothy had some questions about her life and relationships prior to finding herself in Oz. She was seeking to understand feelings she was having about her family and friends and starting to ask questions of those who were closest to her. When she found herself in a new place, she was still struggling with some of those questions. But she was clear on a few things: she valued family, she valued her home and she knew what she wanted.

KNOW THYSELF

In his article, "What is Authentic Leadership (Kruse 2022)," Kevin Kruse describes a more recent theory of leadership that focuses solely on authenticity. He writes, "Authentic leadership theory holds that, in order to be effective, leaders must be authentic to who they are as people and not try to take on a different personality in the name of leadership. Sure, there are skills that all leaders should master—like communication, delegation, and giving feedback. But the theory holds that leaders are actually most effective when they don't try to hide or change who they are deep down."

As leaders, it is so important to know ourselves, our values and our personal goals. As you work to build relationships with your new colleagues, it is critical to begin those relationships being as authentic as possible. Leadership is not a thing to be, it is a thing that we do. Who you are is very different from what you do as a leader.

If you haven't revisited your values and purpose in a while, take an inventory of your core beliefs or ask those who work with you to give you feedback on your strengths and weaknesses. It may seem like this is not the time to be indulgent with "finding yourself" but if you are not sure of who you are, the chaos that is surrounding you (and probably becoming more intense the more you learn and begin to confront it and communicate about it) will quickly consume you. Already, at this point, you may find yourself at times behaving more like the people in the organization than people outside of it. Knowing yourself is grounding and stabilizing not only for you, but for those you work with. You cannot afford to begin reinforcing through your own behavior the chaotic behaviors that you are trying to reduce and eliminate.

Finding a colleague or friend outside of your work or personal life has already been listed as a strategy here, but at this point, there is a more pointed and significant step you can take to find that foundation, if you don't feel you have it. That is finding a counselor, therapist or coach. Although some may think that therapy is for weak-minded individuals who are struggling, nothing could be further from the truth.

An effective counselor will act as a mirror for you. They will reflect back to you what you share to them. They will support you as you learn more about yourself moving through this leadership challenge. Your reactions in a chaotic space, with the pressures that it exerts, are perfect ways to dig more into your core, so that you can interact with your colleagues from a place of authenticity and integrity. A therapist will also help you with recognizing your own patterns of behavior and keep those memories for you. You are learning a lot in your new place and your capacity for this kind of self-learning and discovery will be limited. Take advantage of this incredibly helpful profession.

Your new colleagues are watching your every move. There are many reasons for this, but one is that everyone is looking to find out how you are going to impact their lives, not just their work, but their actual lives. One's occupation impacts families, finances, and personal well-being. They know what *they* need to have happen from you and they will be looking for every indication that you either are going to or not going to be willing or able to do whatever they need you to do. Engaging with these people in an authentic way, leading with real curiosity and with your values at the forefront, will help to build trust in the entire organization.

REFLECT ON YOURSELF AND YOUR INTERACTIONS

You will learn a tremendous amount about yourself the more you engage in chaotic leadership. You will be processing those new insights with many people in your life and hopefully by now, with a therapist. The important thing about any processing you do with yourself or others is that you bring real information to that process. One way to collect useful information for those times is by reflecting on your interactions with specific people or specific situations.

Each time you have any kind of significant interaction with someone during this time, take a minute after to write down some things:

- Who did you engage with?
- What was the purpose of the interaction?
- What energy did the other person bring to the interaction?
- What energy were you feeling or exhibiting before the meeting, during and after?
- Was there a resolution? What kind was it?
- If the interaction was ultimately unproductive, why was that?
- What do you wish you could have done differently or better?

These types of reflections will help you as you explore how you are evolving and will give you information with which to detect patterns. In addition to that, you will have some solid reflections to share with others as you are seeking to build relationships or learn more about yourself.

Your teams are struggling with chaos and everyone should be learning about themselves through that process. But it does little to *tell* people to do this. You need to show them that you take time to do that, as well. And, that you are willing to share with them what you are learning about yourself. This modeling will eventually turn up in other interactions that you have with people as they begin to feel open to share these things about themselves. It becomes a culture of psychological safety and curiosity and that is the culture that you need to have in order to move to a less chaotic and more focused reality.

Finally, ensure that as you learn more about your most successful interactions, you incorporate what you've learned about yourself from those into more of the engagements you have with others. It is not worth the time to reflect if you are not going to analyze the pattern, learn something new and eventually apply it to make sure you are improving your overall results over time.

LOOK IN THE MIRROR

What people see on the outside will be what people come to know and expect of you as their leader:

- Consistency of behavior
- Communication style
- Leadership style
- Values and beliefs
- Physical appearance (attire, attitude)

CONSISTENCY IS CRITICAL

One of the most unsettling and traumatic things about work life can be dealing with an unpredictable colleague. Coming into work each day knowing that this person may be feeling good, and productive and that your relationship may feel alright *or* that they may be negative, depressed, angry or resentful and that your day will turn into an endless, painful and unproductive pity party is exhausting. People who engage with unpredictable people end up perseverating on how they can change or modify themselves, or that person, or their schedules, etc., in order to bring stability to the chaos that person is bringing into their space each day. That is called walking on eggshells and it is not pleasant.

When that unpredictable, inconsistent colleague happens to be your superior, these feelings of walking on eggshells or perseveration cannot only take over your day, but your evenings and weekends, as well. You may find yourself spending inordinate amounts of time analyzing your own behaviors, their emails, their body language, moods, word choices to figure out how they feel about you and whether your position in the organization is safe. This is unproductive and creates drama and sometimes even trauma that is unhealthy for individuals and will inevitably impact everyone in the organization.

As a leader, being consistent is incredibly important. In the article, "Supervisor Support: Does Supervisor Support Buffer or Exacerbate the Adverse Effects of Supervisor Undermining?" (Nahum-Shani 2014), Nahum-Shani, Lim, Henderson, and Vinokur detail findings on three potential negative effects of inconsistent behavior from leadership on employees. First, employees will lack a coherent picture of how well they are doing at their job. This can be not only confusing but cause frustration. Second, employees will feel they have no control over their work environment. Third, employees will have doubts about the quality of their relationship with their supervisor.

An example of inconsistent behavior from a leader might be that an employee finds out that their supervisor has gone behind his back to tell someone else that he has not been doing his job correctly. The employee may feel that he has been doing things correctly and has never heard directly about concerns from the supervisor. Then, within days of hearing that information from a colleague, the supervisor may show up and try to be very "helpful" to the employee, giving them support to do their job. This ends up being very confusing and will lead to immediate mistrust and undermine the relationship.

It's not that you cannot have a bad or "off" day, or change your mind about something, but when you realize that every interaction you have affects those around you, it should be a priority for you to minimize the negative impacts and ensure that you as a work presence is at worst neutral and optimally, inspiring, positive, uplifting and encouraging on a consistent basis. Direct communication in a clear, consistent, kind and respectful manner, should always be a part of this approach, as well.

This is something to reflect on often. Ask your colleagues about your consistency in all aspects of your leadership and talk with your support system about it. If you cannot maintain a consistent demeanor, you will be contributing to the chaos, not calming it.

COMMUNICATION STYLE

As a leader in this new place, take some time to think about what you appreciate about those who communicate with you and why you appreciate them. Think about things like:

- Timing
- Method
- Word Choice
- Tone
- Patterns

Once you have reflected, create some space for you to take those parts that you admire about others' communication styles and apply it to the way you are communicating in your new organization. Look at the ways you have already communicated certain information, has it been consistent with those values that you have established or do you need to make some adjustments? Have you gotten feedback on your communication style and can you incorporate any of that feedback moving forward? Clear, concise communication is kind. Consistently clear, concise and kind communication can be game-changing.

An example of this would be to think about how you answer emails. Do you answer them late at night? Even though this may be your only time to sit and do that, what message is it sending to your colleagues? Could it be signaling to them that you value a late-night work ethic? Is that what you want and is it productive for you? Or, would it be better to answer the email whenever you can, but schedule it to go out during work hours?

Also, what do you do with questions that you get in emails? Do you answer that email with more questions which results in a lot of back and forth or do you call or visit that person to engage in a conversation so that you can ensure you understand exactly what they are asking and answer any follow up questions they have right there? Would this help both of you in terms of email workload?

Think about information that needs to be communicated. Are you doing that primarily during meeting times? Or are you utilizing technology like collaborative and consistently updated online hubs so that you can use your meeting times for real dialogue, connection and problem solving?

Think about how you are presenting yourself at meetings. Where do you sit? How do you sit? Are your arms crossed, are you the notetaker and facilitator? Are you distracted? What are these things communicating to your team? Is this what you want? Are any of your behaviors being mirrored by your colleagues?

These are some of the things to think about when determining your communication style. Your verbal, nonverbal, and written communication styles are the primary vehicles for connection and it is worth taking some time to think about what you want those things to say about you and ultimately what you want to model for your colleagues as you move through this change process.

LEADERSHIP STYLE

Many leaders have been through some schooling or certification programs to become leaders and have done some visioning about the type of leader they would like to be. Now is a good time to revisit that, or engage in the process if you haven't already. There is certainly research easily available to any leader who wants to explore this, and it is worthwhile to dig into this a little bit at this point in your journey.

Again, you can begin with your own reflections on yourself since you arrived at your new post. What type of a leader have you been? If you have been following along with some of these strategies, you have been a learner, collaborator, and communicator. You will be building relationships and listening a lot.

If you are picking up this book after having been somewhere for a while, then this may not be true for various reasons. It may not be that you are not doing these things because you haven't wanted to, but because the chaos has prevented you from remembering who you want to be as a leader. Take the time to think about the leader that everyone engages with every day. Who are you? Who do you want to be? What is the gap between those two pictures and how can you get support to become the type of leader you admire?

PERSONAL VALUES AND BELIEFS

This has already been addressed here, but should be consistently reviewed. As a learner, some of these pieces may evolve over time based on the needs that you discover in your organization or as the landscape of the work changes. One thing is clear, it is not necessarily *what* your values and beliefs are, but more *how* consistent and clear you are about those that matter to the organization. These should be held up and demonstrated in your interactions with everyone, and come through in what you share about yourself. If they don't, your people may struggle to know why you are making certain decisions and where these decisions may be leading them as part of the organization.

PERSONAL APPEARANCE

Although it may seem superficial to discuss this, personal appearance is an important aspect of who you are in the organization and it will impact others. This is not about some type of beauty ideal or fashion, but it is about what your personal appearance communicates about you as an individual. Casual, formal, stylish, professional, eccentric—whether we like it or not, we are judged on these things. It is important to be aware of what your personal style says about you as an individual and that it matches what you want it to say. You may not think it is important but others notice.

As a new leader, you are establishing credibility at a very vulnerable time in your organization. It may not be the best time to challenge the organization's beliefs about what a leader should look like. Formality, thought it may not be your personal style, might help to support your reputation as a leader for now.

As another example, a leader who dresses well and styles their hair differently every day may be communicating attention to detail and a wish to present a well put together personality. Some may perceive this as a positive. Some, especially in a chaotic place where people are just barely surviving, may interpret this as the leader not being stressed out or having a lot of time on their hands to shop and get ready in the morning.

As a leader, you may be getting up an hour or two every day to ensure that you exercise, meditate and attend to your personal dress and grooming and the idea of having extra time may be laughable to you. However, if you aren't aware of some of these messages that your appearance could be communicating, you will be unprepared when you are portrayed this way or your relationships are negatively impacted by those perceptions.

Awareness is key here. You do not need to change your appearance necessarily, but you should be intentional about it. As has been discussed many times, be aware of it, discuss it or ask questions about it from people you trust and adjust based on what you hear, if you need to. If you are a leader who thinks about personal appearance a lot already and perhaps worries about things that you cannot change that you would like to change, take heart here, as well. A number of studies have shown that leadership presence is more affected by body positioning (how you hold space in a room) and your tone of voice.

Your colleagues will come to know who you are based on what you do and what you say. Reflect often on if you are contributing intentionally to your style in a way that you are comfortable with. If you are not comfortable with what people are coming to expect from you, then take steps to change it and be honest with those around you about how you plan to change, why you are making that change and what you hope that it does to benefit them and the work of the organization as a whole. This type of attention and awareness to how you present yourself as a leader can pay huge dividends in your relationships, the sense of trust that you build and the types of conversations you are able to have as a leader in your new place.

YOU DO YOU

Once you have been intentional and thought through these aspects of your personality and leadership, revisit consistency and intention. It is of utmost importance that you do not let the chaos of this new place change the core aspects of you. Exhibiting certain types of behaviors, communicating in certain ways, dressing in certain ways, that are aligned with the patterns that existed in the organization prior to your arrival may not be the best ways to show that you value your new colleagues and respect them.

In fact, assimilating to the chaos will be scary for some people and considered a victory for others. Some of the first people to notice this, will be those in your personal life. If anyone at home starts to notice that you are changing, listen to them. Reflect and decide if that is really what you intended to have happen.

Respect and trust will come from your new colleagues getting to know you as an authentic and integrated person who can maintain who you are even in very uncertain times. Assimilation is not appreciation and it will ultimately limit your ability to keep your perspective as the organization's leader and not just another one of the employees.

REFLECTION QUESTIONS FOR YOUR ACTION PLAN

- Have you completed any personality or leadership inventories?
- If you have, have you revisited them recently?
- If you haven't, would doing that be helpful to you as you think about what you want your style to be and what matches with the strong aspects of your personality and beliefs?
- Have you received feedback in the past that may be related to how you are presenting yourself at work?
- Have you solicited feedback in this area from your stakeholders?
- Do you see any of your personal attributes being mirrored or discussed in the organization?
- What kind of impact is it having?

SELF-MANAGEMENT PLANNING AND REFLECTION

- Do you have someone in your life that you can trust to be honest with you about what you are communicating through your style and personality?
- Is it time to go shopping for some new shoes?
- That's always a good idea.

A RESOURCE FROM THE FIELD

In their book, *99 Ways to Lead and Succeed* (Bush 1st edition 2013), Howard Bultinck and Lynn Bush share practical strategies to be more effective leaders from their many years of experience at various levels of school leadership. They explore everything from moral and ethical leadership practices, to dealing with the everyday stresses of school leadership and how to literally stay alive through the many pressures that school leaders experience. This book is easy to navigate through and pick up anytime you need a practical way to adjust an area of your leadership style that isn't working for you or your organization.

A RESOURCE FROM THE OUTFIELD

Glennon Doyle's podcast, *We Can Do Hard Things* (Doyle 2021), offers women the opportunity to think through how they are impacted by cultural norms in society and historical issues concerning women in all aspects of society. The conversations are thought-provoking and supportive to women grappling with all kinds of issues, both personal and professional. A leader contemplating her impact and how to be thoughtful and intentional regarding it, may find this podcast helpful in terms of awareness of how she has been impacted personally, without even knowing it, and how she may in turn, be impacting those around her.

CASE STUDY ON WEARING YOUR RUBY SLIPPERS: FINDING DOROTHY

Situation

A female central office administrator, who had been an educational leader for over ten years, realized that she was feeling unsure of her next steps in her career, anxious about her life and questioning her purpose as a leader. She had been working in one area of the district office for some time and had experienced working under many different superintendents. While she was feeling fulfilled to some extent in that role, she wanted to explore moving into the Superintendency. But she had not received encouragement from others that that was a job that would be fulfilling for her or worse, that taking a job like that would mean misery for the remainder of her career.

She was feeling trapped and confused in that aspect of her life, and also began to recognize that there were other parts of her life that were making things at work difficult to manage. She was struggling as a wife and a mother and had lost touch with her friends and family. The struggles were becoming apparent to those she worked with and others started encouraging her to seek counseling. That was embarrassing for her as she had always prided herself on being someone that others could trust for support. Now that she was finding herself needing that support, she began experiencing a crisis of conscience.

Overarching Challenge

This experienced leader needed to explore who she was at this point in her life, make changes necessary to move forward in her leadership and feel more grounded in her life, and then be as secure as possible in those decisions so that she could actually love and support those who needed her.

The Cost of Not Finding a Solution

Many times women find themselves in the situation where they are supporting everyone else in their lives and have little to no time left for the support of their own well-being. This superhero syndrome may feel good in the sense that they are "doing" everything they should do, but in reality, it feels terrible. Not attending to the feelings that naturally arise when someone doesn't pay attention to their emotional wellness, their struggles and their ambitions for their own life, can have catastrophic consequences.

Mental and physical health are the only true wealth we have in this world. With those intact, we can find ways to accomplish other goals. Without them, there is no hope. To continue working and living in a state of confusion, fear or anxiety is not only detrimental to one's own emotional and physical health, it does nothing for those that the individual struggles to support.

In this case, this experienced leader could not continue without a change. Whether she decided to stay in this position or ones like it, or whether she decided to move forward and become a Superintendent, she would have to grapple with the reasons that she found herself ineffective at that point and needing so much support in her day-to-day life.

Solution

At the behest of her colleagues and trusted friends, she found herself a counselor and began to explore the areas of her life that were most troubling. Through this work she made some tough decisions about her personal life, that while difficult, were necessary for her to be a good mother and a healthy individual. This process was difficult, but with the support of her counselor, friends, and by reconnecting purposefully with her family of origin, she was able to make those changes. As her personal life began to feel more balanced and peaceful, she could shift her focus to who she was at work and what she really wanted.

Enlisting the help of mentors in the field, she reflected with them on what it would mean to stay in her current role for the remainder of her career and what it would mean to move into a different role. She deliberately chose people to talk with who were successful at the Superintendency or other central office roles and finding meaning in their roles so that they can share the positives of both pathways.

She took time to reflect on feedback that she had received recently and not so recently at work to determine who others saw when they interacted with her. Her inventory took into account everything from how her office was arranged, to the nonverbal body language she used when she was in conversation, to how she dressed. She began to be more thoughtful about these very simple, but very powerful indicators of her personality to the outside world.

She decided after all of this, that she would like to make a change in her role and began to feel more confident every day that she might be able to make a positive difference for a school district in the role of Superintendent. While she didn't get the first position she applied for (it's actually the 8th position that she received), each time she interviewed she felt more sure that she was headed in the right direction.

As a new Superintendent, she continues to think about who she is, how she is changing as a person in this new role, and what she wants to present to others. In this new phase of her journey, she feels grounded and ready for the future and while there are always struggles, she continues to use her strategies and supports to reflect often and stay healthy emotionally and physically.

She has now incorporated these types of mental health supports into her work with other administrators and staff, ensuring that as professionals, a focus on mental health and well-being is maintained for the benefit of the students that are served in her district.

Chapter 6

Confront the Lions, Tigers, and Bears

"True courage is facing danger when you are afraid."

—*The Wizard of Oz*

As a new leader, you have been learning a lot about your new organization. You have been transparent about what you have learned, you have turned some lights on and are being collaborative about where you think you can move forward together and what are the most pressing issues. You are working with your teams to make decisions together and your plans are probably starting to come together.

As an individual, you are also learning a lot about yourself. You have taken a lot of time to journal and reflect, you have been asking a lot of questions and listening a lot. You have been thinking about your actions and various aspects of your style and how those are contributing to your leadership personality and maybe you've even found some time to shop (always fun) and reinvent some aspects of who you are.

Through this process, hopefully, you are discovering new alliances and finding that you have folks supporting you as you work to lead this new place out of the tornado and to the Emerald City. Your journey is certainly rocky, but you are still moving forward. It shouldn't surprise you that on this journey there are some scary characters. From the time you began this quest, as has been discussed, people have been watching you. They have been listening and while your time has probably been taken up by those folks who were quick out of the gate to come and talk with you and share what has been upsetting to you, there are those who have been waiting quietly and patiently to make their entrance into your story.

They have probably been gathering information, talking to others and building up for a really impactful interaction that may threaten your progress towards your goals. This warning is not intended to create a sense of paranoia, but it is intended to help you see around some dark corners. Unfortunately, social media and electronic communication platforms have made it easy to "confront" someone with anger, rage and negativity without actually looking them in the eyes. The more negative the feedback, the higher the chance that you will receive it in your inbox or voicemail, or read it online instead of being faced with it in-person.

If you have been following the strategies, you will be prepared for how to respond to his type of feedback through interactions that are filled with real information, honesty and engagement. As a person who is really grounded in herself and her beliefs, you will be able to approach and respond with authenticity and integrity, kindness and respect. Don't be surprised or scared when these new folks come out of the forest, just be prepared and get ready to engage authentically and productively.

PROACTIVELY PROTECT YOUR TIME

In her article, "4 Ways Leaders Can Protect Their Time and Empower Their Employees" (Thomas 2018), Maura Thomas argues that a leader's most important job is reflective thinking time. This type of time is when a leader can prepare for crises, or plan thoughtfully for the future. When you are leading an organization in chaos, you need to have time each day to proactively plan for your next move, as well as, be able to respond thoughtfully to what is occurring in real-time, which are often difficult conversations and interactions.

In order to prepare before difficult interactions happen, there are some things that you can do ahead of time. First, make sure that you have empty space in your calendar every week. When these situations arise, you need to have time to think and thoughtfully respond. If your calendar is jam-packed from the time you walk in the door until late at night, you will find yourself under water with angry people quickly.

If you need to put *everything* on the calendar in order to protect the time, then do that. Estimate more time for meetings than are planned and schedule time for emails, phone calls and walking around. Not only does that help to keep those items which are important, top of mind, it will also build space into your work day to address emergency conversations when they arise.

Also, remember that you are in a very chaotic place. Any opportunity to limit surprises and create predictability and space for you to think should be taken advantage of. If you have an administrative assistant, make the time to talk about how that person can have access to your emails and answer those that can be answered for you, draft responses for you to those the assistant doesn't feel totally comfortable answering or give you a heads-up when there is an email in there that is likely to be upsetting.

By doing this, you are maximizing his support to you and also, giving yourself time to prepare before reading something that could potentially throw you off your game. How would you prepare? If you haven't tried mindful meditation or breathing techniques yet, you have permission to skip to the next chapter now.

If you don't have an administrative assistant dedicated to you, or that person is not someone you trust, then it is time to take a look at those aspects of your organization and how you might be able to address that now. You need support. Find someone in the organization who can help with that, or begin working on securing an additional person for yourself.

Also, consider not answering your direct phone line. By having your administrative assistant answer your phone for you, you will again provide the opportunity to screen some more of your interactions. It is important for you to protect your time and your mental health, these are important strategies to consider as you are new here and now is the time to set that tone. Eventually, you may feel comfortable doing these things yourself, but for now, don't feel bad asking for that support.

Your days are very busy right now. You are not just learning anymore, you are engaging in real planning and reflection. You are walking around and interacting with people. When you are taken by surprise with an angry phone call or email from someone who was not even on your radar at such a vulnerable time, your first instinct may be to shut your computer down and crawl under your desk. Accusations, personal attacks, attempts to make you feel unsafe in your position will all happen. It is your response that matters the most. And yes, you must respond, at least once. The healthier you are and the more time you have at your disposal to respond, the better.

INVITE BEFORE YOU RESPOND

When an angry email or phone call comes in, read it or listen carefully and respond that you need some time to answer thoughtfully and then take a break. Responding in a moment of fear or anger will most definitely cause you to do or say something you will ultimately regret. Close your computer, put down your phone, stand up and take a deep breath. Close your eyes and remember that in this moment you are safe and you can take the time you need to think about what you just read or heard and respond thoughtfully.

When you are ready to respond, consider if you can meet with or talk with that person on the phone. Invite this person to a conversation instead of answering their correspondence with a defensive posture. Many times, this act of invitation and bravery helps immediately to create a sense that you care to listen and engage.

If you are able to engage that person in a live conversation, make sure you listen for as long as you can. You may find that the conversation starts out difficult, but if you can maintain the same curious and listening posture that you have been demonstrating since you arrived, the conversation may begin to settle into a solution orientation, which is where you want to be.

If you cannot continue to listen because the conversation is going on too long, or because the tone has become dangerous or disrespectful, politely but firmly interrupt and say that you will need to reschedule the rest of the conversation for a time when either you have more of your schedule free, or when the conversation can be respectful and productive. Either way, whether the conversation takes a positive turn and you can begin to problem solve, or if it continues to be unproductive and you need to end the meeting or call without resolution, build in time for yourself within 24 hours to write your notes and decide your next steps.

CONVERSATIONS ARE BETTER

If you cannot arrange a face to face or a phone call and you are forced to respond in writing, realize that this type of correspondence can then be made public and may be available for anyone to read at any time, given the discretion of your angry stakeholder. Answer only the questions that are asked, and ensure that two people have read your response before you send it.

Do your diligence to ensure that your communication does not reveal protected information and that you have consulted your attorney if you feel there are legal matters at play. At this time in your journey, anything you write is subject to *mass dissemination*, whether it is on social media, through email or right to local or national press. You may want to engage the help of a communications consultant if you do not have that position in your district or school. These folks can support you with social media inventories, advice for your responses and follow up reflection support.

While consistent responses are best if multiple people decide to express their discontent at the same time, they can also be seen as "form communications" and be attacked for that. Conversations over the phone or in-person are always better if you can have them, in these cases, as well.

Finally, if after engaging once there doesn't seem to be any way to resolve the issue and the same questions continue to be asked of you, let your last communication indicate that you have answered the questions asked, the answer will not be changing and that you will no longer be addressing that same question. Sometimes disengaging is the only way to stop a back-and-forth pattern that ultimately robs you of time and energy to continue the good work you are doing.

KEEP REFLECTING

When you have situations like this arise, reflect on what, if anything, these interactions tell you about the current state of the organization. Are these interactions intended to keep the chaos going to hide or protect parts of the organization that are unhealthy? This is why it is critical that you not ignore these seemingly very distracting and upsetting interactions, they will help you learn more. In the best of cases, you will form some more helpful relationships and gain some new insights. In the worst case, you have a headache and take some personal time the next day to regroup. Use your support networks and protect your mental health. These conversations and interactions can take a toll faster than most aspects of leadership.

REFLECTION QUESTIONS FOR YOUR ACTION PLAN

- What patterns are emerging in the organization when you engage in these difficult conversations?
- Is there anything about your personal style of communication or leadership that needs adjusting in order to proactively address any of the concerns that are being communicated?
- Are there individuals in your organization who are contributing to the information being brought to you in these interactions? Do you need to have some internal conversations?
- Are any of these concerns related to your transparency or lack thereof? Can you make any adjustments there?
- Are communications taking over your time to do your work and can hiring someone internally or externally help you to take this responsibility off your plate?

SELF-MANAGEMENT PLANNING AND REFLECTION

- When you have been confronted with anger and critical feedback in the past, what has been your reaction?
- Do you engage in difficult conversations in your personal life?
- If you are avoiding them, why is that?

- Have you discussed your approach to these situations with your therapist, counselor or coach?
- If you don't have a therapist or counselor yet, what are you waiting for?

A RESOURCE FROM THE FIELD

Ultimately, the goal of having hard conversations is not just to ensure that you don't make others more angry by ignoring them, it's to gather good information, build trust and develop working relationships during a very difficult time. In *Asking the Right Questions: A Guide to Continuous Improvement with Stakeholder Input* (Burden 2019), Stu Silberman and Gay Burden can provide a school leader with key questions to utilize in order to establish a collective vision for improvement. This easy to implement framework can support many types of conversations, even difficult ones.

A RESOURCE FROM THE OUTFIELD

Brené Brown's *Atlas of the Heart* (Brown, *Atlas of the Heart: Mapping Meaningful Connection and the Language of Human Experience* 1st Edition 2021) is a reference/storybook that can be critically beneficial to anyone looking to identify emotions and experiences in any situation. The reason this is selected as a resource for this section, is that many times when faced with difficult conversations like those outlined in this chapter, it is easy for the new leader to mistake many different types of emotions for pure anger.

Often when people in chaotic environments are expressing difficult feelings, what sounds like anger is actually disappointment, shame, fear, etc. A new leader armed with a way to interpret these emotions with more granularity will not only be able to more quickly ask the right questions, but will also be able to validate more specific concerns and navigate toward better solutions.

CASE STUDY ENGAGING WITH THE LIONS, TIGERS AND BEARS: CONFRONTING THE NEED FOR CHANGE

Situation

A principal with a couple of years of experience is transferred into a new building in her district. She knows that the building has just lost their long-time principal and that he had been successful there for many years, having especially trusting relationships with the staff. However, in the last couple of years, the make-up of the student body had significantly shifted. The building had a new population of second language learners who were struggling in the very traditional courses and instructional environments that were continuing to be offered.

What had worked for years was now not working for many students and the staff were feeling frustrated and overwhelmed, although not feeling like they needed to change their practices. In fact, they were very much convinced that they just needed to have more teachers in the building to address the student changes, or more and different programs to support the "different students." This new principal wasn't interviewed, but appointed, and the staff were feeling that they had lost an opportunity to choose who they felt would be best for the building and the current challenges.

As her first year began, and she started to audit instruction and systems, she found that there was very little attention being paid to student interests, language support or family and parental support. There were a few staff members who were trying to convince their colleagues of the need for these issues to be addressed, but overwhelmingly the staff felt that doing anything different than they had been doing was not going to help. They felt that students and parents were just very different than they had been in the past.

As the principal began to have conversations with staff members about updating their practices, she was met with a "doubling down" on outdated practices and consequences for students. Staff became defensive and started to grade students more harshly and insist that students were given consequences for their inattentive behaviors and lack of attention to due dates. She felt the culture spiraling quickly out of her control and had fewer and fewer allies each day she walked into the building.

Overarching Challenge

To update the effectiveness of staff instructional strategies and align them with the needs of the students in the building while addressing the toxic culture of student-blaming.

The Cost of Not Finding a Solution

Change is scary for everyone, especially those who need to change in order to be effective. When these changes are transformational in nature, they are layered and require a commitment to learning, making mistakes and trying again. A new leader needing to quickly begin this type of transformational change must be set up for success in every way possible.

In this situation, the leader came in with some strikes against her. One is that she was not interviewed by her new colleagues. While her superior had complete confidence in her ability to lead, staff were using this as an excuse to not embrace her and instead focus on everything they felt she was doing wrong. Another was that the previous leader had not even begun to address the changing student population, and instead spent his final years praising the staff and supporting and encouraging them in the face of all the challenges that were impacting them as a building.

This new leader could simply have walked in and begun doing the same, supporting and encouraging the staff and may have won more fans in the process. However, the cost of doing that would be that students would continue to be underserved; students who needed the support and effective instruction more than anyone. Additionally, by ignoring ineffective practice right from the start, her credibility was at risk as a true instructional leader.

Solution

As soon as she realized that her initial conversations were ineffective and were actually leading staff to enforce even more punitive actions against the struggling students, the principal began to enlist the help of some district office support. The goal was to initially comprehensively audit instruction and identify the teachers who needed to adjust the most. Data were used in this process, as well, and classes with the most students falling behind were flagged as needing support.

Then she began bringing students in to speak with her about their experiences in classrooms. Students were reporting that they felt completely disrespected and uncomfortable in some cases in these classrooms. They pointed to specific incidents in which they tried to speak with their parents or teachers about this, but were met with disbelief or consequences for reporting their feelings and being disrespectful to their teachers.

After collecting her data, she began to bring teachers in one at a time to allow them to tell her what they were struggling with, but also to share what she had been learning from the students. She began with the teachers who were most upset that she was hired. In these conversations, she listened first, made sure that she understood their concerns, and then shared with them the concerns she had about their practices and data.

She was direct and respectful, but firm and clear about her expectations. Initially, staff were upset by the conversations. However, the staff members who had been trying to have these conversations with their teams for a few years and were already trying to improve, began to feel more empowered as teachers began to share what was being said to them individually. The messages were reinforced then, in team meetings, as those who were eager for a change felt they could advocate for their students more strongly.

Coupled with these difficult conversations (some which had to take place more than a few times) the new principal also became more vigilant about noticing what *was* going right and offering copious praise and encouragement. *But only* when things were going right or were improving. She was cautious not to encourage anything that was mediocre or that wasn't specifically addressing the new focus of the building, which was simply to ensure that instruction was tailored to the needs of the students who were there at that time, not those who were there in the past.

The culture began to shift and some teachers decided that they were not interested in changing. Some of them retired early and some pursued other positions. Most teachers began to appreciate the feedback, both constructive and positive and genuinely became interested in learning more about how they could be more effective. The principal was generous with her time and coaching and the building found that it made significant gains in student achievement and growth in only a few short years. The direct and difficult conversations, informed by real data and observations (especially those of the students), were a critical jumping off point to this transformational change.

Chapter 7

Rely on Your Brain, Your Heart, Some Courage, and a Lot of Hard Work

"You are capable of more than you know."

—*Glinda*

Much has been written on healthy work-life balance and there are many strategies for maintaining said balance during stressful times. This chapter is not intended to suggest ways to keep work and life in balance when you are leading an organization struck by a tornado of chaos and dysfunction. In reality, when one is put in this type of leadership position, you must work more than you'd like to. If you are committed to the work, then this will be your new normal, at least for a while.

You have many people depending on you to diagnose, create a plan and build trust quickly. It will not be a secret that you are working hard. You should be working hard to listen, learn, strategize, stabilize your organization and your own emotions, refine and clarify your leadership and communication style, and handle very difficult and sometimes emotionally intense conversations and interactions. It won't always be like this if you are successful in moving toward a new, more calm sense of normalcy, but at the beginning, your life will be unbalanced and tilted toward work more than you'd like.

To revisit our friend Dorothy, she's been on the yellow brick road for some time now learning and engaging. She's been scared, sleepy, frustrated and curious. She's still leading. And, she still hasn't reached her goal of getting home. In a sense, this journey of hers is our journey as leaders. When we begin somewhere, it is not our home yet. Even in a functioning and well-established organization, we have a lot of learning to do to feel at home.

In a chaotic organization, not only do you begin feeling like an outsider, you may also find that the intensity of the work makes you feel like you are longing for your old place of work, or your own home and family in a way that you haven't before. One of the goals of this journey is to make your new organization feel like home for everyone (including yourself) and to get back, literally and figuratively, to your own home and family in a way that is balanced and filled with new insights about yourself as a person.

HAVE A TALK WITH YOURSELF

You are engaging in really difficult work and have been on the road for a while. Reflect on the time you have spent and where you have spent the time. What amount of time, if any, has been spent on the maintenance of your emotional well-being. Time with your counselor, coach or therapist (yes, you should definitely have one by now) should count in this analysis. However, there are other tools that you will need along this journey to stay mentally fit and healthy enough to lead. Some questions to ask yourself now are:

- Am I meeting my own basic needs?
- Do I eat?
- Do I eat healthy foods?
- Am I engaging in emotionally or physically harmful behaviors?
- Am I sleeping enough?
- Where in my day do I or can I get movement into my schedule?
- Do I feel connected with my purpose?
- Do I feel that I am acting in alignment with my values?
- Am I aware of how I am feeling and when I am experiencing negative or harmful emotions, do I have strategies to support my thoughts?
- Am I maintaining my connection and obligations with those I love?

This is not a self-help chapter and as stated above, there are many books and podcasts that are devoted entirely to this subject, but there is one aspect of self-management that is of critical importance to leaders in chaos. Cultivating a practice of mindful meditation can truly transform a leader and provide a way to manage stress and emotions that will sustain through times of intense stress. This practice is just that, taking a little time each day or sometimes multiple times a day, to pause and become aware of your mind and body.

Much like developing a bigger and better vocabulary of emotions, a leader should find ways to develop a better and more accurate vocabulary of herself. Learning to recognize your reactions to various situations either in your mind or body, can allow you to step outside of yourself and your gut reactions to be more thoughtful and less impulsive. Mindfulness can help with catastrophic thinking, or thought spirals that predict the worst versions of the future. It can help with anxious thoughts as an ineffective coping mechanism. Mindfulness can bring peace and clarity to even the most difficult situations.

There are many apps, books and podcasts on this subject with tools to help you begin your journey of mindfulness. Once you see the benefits of this physically and emotionally, you will want to incorporate it more for those you work with, as well. There isn't anyone in a chaotic place who won't find mindfulness a helpful support to their well-being.

HAVE A TALK WITH YOUR LOVED ONES

Early in this book, it was suggested to talk with your loved ones about how to maintain your relationships now that you have discovered the magnitude of the work before you in this new place. Even if you were able to have that conversation early in the process, it is important to continue to come back to it regularly. It is normal for everyone to lose track of commitments you've made when you are working in such a chaotic environment. At this point, as you are hopefully beginning to reap some of the benefits of the hard work you have been doing, the conversations with your loved ones can revolve around establishing non-negotiables so that you can continue to stay connected.

What is important to your family right now? You are and have been probably overextended with the work you have been doing. What have you missed? What are they missing out of your relationships? Where are the opportunities to create new traditions and rituals? A start to this discussion might be, "I love you all so much, and this job is really intense. I need you to know that you are very important to me and while I'm making decisions about what I need to prioritize at work, I want to work around *our* priorities as a family (or group of friends)."

Items to discuss:

- Weeknight routines
- Weekend rituals
- Date nights
- Events with children
- Extended family obligations
- Religious obligations

What are the things that are really important, and what are the *nice-to-haves*? If you know something is really important, you can make that a priority as often as possible. Knowing the nice-to-haves is imperative, because those will be the unexpected surprises that fill up the emotional bank accounts of your loved ones when you are able to schedule them in. You might find out that there are some things you are participating in that are not so important to the people you love and that could be a relief for you, as well.

ASK FOR HELP

Your loved ones (and your counselor) are not the only people who can help you maintain as healthy a balance as possible right now. Your senior leadership team and administrative support team members can also support you in very impactful ways with this aspect of leadership. Asking for support from these folks is a win-win proposition. Not only are you receiving support on a critical aspect of your well-being that will ultimately impact your ability to lead, but you are modeling for your team members a commitment to self-care that you want to see from them.

Your team is only as good as its weakest member. The smaller your team, the more of an impact one unhealthy individual can have on your organization. It is a strategic imperative for you and your team to attend to your mental health and wellness. Here are some ways you can help each other:

- Remind each other that mindfulness and reflection should be built into team times and meeting agendas.
- Take meetings and conversations on the road, walk and talk.
- Look at each other's office and work spaces, where can furniture be adjusted to support more movement or even rest? Do people need a standing desk? Are there comfortable chairs?
- Support remote work opportunities for each other when presence is not essential on-site.
- Stay focused on purpose and support each other by encouraging the elimination of nonessential work and activities that are not supportive of the overall improvement of the organization.
- Help each other avoid "remodeling the kitchen" and tinkering with things in the organization that may make work "prettier" but will not result in actual change.
- Learn about each other's families and personal interests. Support the development of those interests and the obligations that you have to your loved ones.

KEEP YOUR CALENDAR PUBLIC

The goal of this strategy is not to elicit sympathy, but to ensure that everyone can see what you are spending time on. Keeping your priority work items on your calendar, building in time and space for reflection and new learning, for engaging with your stakeholders, for working on communication, helps to enlighten your colleagues as to what your job entails, what you consider a priority and how much work it is actually taking to lead the organization.

In an effort to maintain a consistent attitude and promote a sense of fun and balance in an organization, sometimes leaders will downplay the amount of work they are doing to "keep things light." Unfortunately, while this type of leader may find this a helpful strategy in a functioning place, this type of leader can be perceived as someone who really "doesn't have much to do," in a place plagued by chaos.

This is so damaging, not only for the leader, but for the health and future of the organization. By not presenting a realistic and hopefully healthy picture of what type of leadership the organization is requiring, there is the potential for the stakeholders to mistakenly believe that the position is unnecessary or to begin to undervalue it.

For everyone involved, knowing that leadership has a tremendous impact on the overall success of any organization, it is important that the value of the leader is clear and that her work never becomes underestimated in the eyes of all the stakeholders. This is not to say that fun doesn't have a place. This will be addressed in the next chapter. However, what you are trying to do is very serious, very time-consuming, very thoughtful and deliberate work. It is critical that everyone understands that.

COMMUNICATE REGULARLY

Finally, ensure that your communication plan that we have already worked on, includes opportunities for you to regularly provide updates on your work and the overall state of the organization as your understanding evolves. Communication like this:

- helps to keep all stakeholders up-to-date
- serves as documentation of your process
- supports your own evidence of success
- ensures you take focused time to reflect, analyze and summarize how your experience of leadership is progressing

If your work-life balance is going to be off for a while, it's important for people to recognize that this is a sacrifice that you are making right now and they should know what you are learning and how you are using that learning to lead.

FIND YOUR BALANCE

All this being said, continue to have conversations with yourself, your counselor, your colleagues, and especially your loved ones about how soon you will be able to restore yourself to a more balanced life. You will not be able to sustain an unbalanced life like this for long. In fact, we know now that chronic stress reduces our life expectancy by years (Welfare 2020), not months or days. Reducing and ultimately eliminating the stress that comes from leading an organization in this kind of chaos should be happening by the end of the first year. If there is not reduction of stress in any area by the end of your first year, it may be time to rethink the longevity you can expect to have in this position.

Slowly, begin to schedule in more time for the things that you know you need as an individual, more times to get to the "nice-to-haves" and more time for your colleagues to attend to the other aspects of their lives. If you are going to restore calm and peace, it will only come to the degree that you and your colleagues can restore their whole lives to calm and peace, as well.

REFLECTIONS FOR YOUR ACTION PLAN

- Are you giving grace to those around you who have not figured out this balance in their life, which may be impacting your own ability to do so?
- If not, have you intentionally had a conversation to problem solve that issue?
- Is your calendar reflective of how you spend your time?
- Is your calendar reflective of how you *want* to spend your time?

SELF-MANAGEMENT PLANNING AND REFLECTION

- As you are working to negotiate with your loved ones around finding a balance during this difficult time, how are you encouraging others to do that, too?
- Are you finding ways to reward or incentivize yourself to keep to your personal health habits and non-negotiable commitments?

- Are you giving yourself permission to make mistakes in this area, and start again the next day?
- How is your mindset?
- What are the stories you have in your mind regarding work/life blend or balance?
- Are the stories true or are they old scripts from your family, friends or coworkers from the past?
- Have you taken some time to reflect on your values in this area and how your early life has impacted these?

A RESOURCE FROM THE FIELD

Caryn Wells describes ways that school leaders can utilize mindfulness to not only reduce stress but also become more effective leaders in her book, *Mindfulness: How School Leaders can Reduce Stress and Thrive on the Job* (Wells Reprint Edition 2016). Now more than ever, school leaders need to find practical ways to integrate this practice into their school and home lives in order to cope with the incredible pressures of this profession.

A RESOURCE FROM THE OUTFIELD

The app *Calm* (Calm 2021), provides a vast library of resources to support mindfulness and meditation practices. Offering everything from daily meditations to support for sleep, stress and anxiety and even bedtime stories, this app is a very useful tool for any leader looking to begin to incorporate this work into their lives.

Chapter 8

Laugh, Even When the Wicked Witch Is on Your Tail

"I shall take the heart, for brains do not make one happy and happiness is the best thing in the world."

—*Tin Man*

Wherever you are in your leadership journey at this point, take this moment to pause and think about the role that laughter plays in your life:

- When do you laugh (really laugh)?
- Who or what makes you laugh?
- Do you laugh with your loved ones?
- Do you laugh with your colleagues?
- Is there laughter in your schools or in your district office?
- Do your students laugh every day?

If these are difficult questions to think about, take a moment to consider these questions:

- What are your perceptions of people who laugh regularly?
- What are your perceptions of people who never seem to laugh?
- How would it feel to laugh more?
- What would it feel like if people judged you based on how much or how little you laughed and would you care?

The truth is that laughter needs to play a much more important role in all of our lives for various reasons. According to the Mayo Clinic (Staff 2021), laughter has tremendous shortterm and long-term effects:

- Stimulates important organs like the heart, lungs and muscles
- Activates and relieves your stress response (in a good and healthy way)
- Soothes tension
- Improves your immune system
- Relieves pain (not just emotional pain, but the physical kind, too!)
- Increases overall personal satisfaction with your day, week, month, life
- Improves your mood

However, one of the most important things about laughter is that it feels good. Laughing releases stress. It's a physical response to a pleasurable experience (most of the time) and it plays a critical role in how our brain processes the moment at hand. In leadership positions where there is chaos all around us, it may not feel appropriate to laugh all the time. It may feel like laughter is not going to help anyone, but instead will lead to a perception that you are not taking your situation seriously enough. However, there are many good reasons to laugh with those you work with and with those you lead, because they will experience all the positive effects right along with you. And, laughing is especially important during difficult times.

BUT, ARE YOU FUNNY?

Before discussing the whys and hows of leadership humor, you might be wondering if you are a funny person. If you are not sure, now would be a good time to ask some trusted friends and colleagues if they think you are funny. You might consider asking when you are most funny and if you are really feeling like you can be vulnerable, what makes people laugh about you when you are *not* in the room.

Please recognize that as the leader, there are people who will want to make sure they fulfill any and all of your expectations of them, no matter how they *actually* feel about it. They may be laughing with you when you are around, even if you're not being funny! It would be great for folks you work with to let you know what things are funny about you when you are trying to be funny and when you are not trying to be funny.

You may be thinking to yourself that you aren't funny because you don't tell jokes at work. But leadership humor doesn't have to be about jokes. In fact, if you rely only on actual jokes in your humor arsenal, you need to be very good at reading the body language around you after delivering the punchline. Make sure that the laughter you hear is authentic. If it feels or looks forced, you might want to scale back on that. If they aren't laughing but groaning and smiling, they might just be tolerating you. Not all people can deliver jokes well, and not all jokes are funny to everyone.

But the good news is that laughter doesn't have to come from jokes. Finding humor in everyday situations, especially when you can make fun of yourself or something you have done, can be the best way to get folks giggling. Just ensure that you are practicing self-awareness. There may be some people on your team that appreciate your kind of humor and some people who will laugh simply because they think you need or want them to. Spend some time around your folks to get a sense of when laughter is genuine for them. What does it sound like? If you pay attention, you will be able to tell the difference.

The last thing you want is for people to dread having you around because you expect them to laugh at everything you say. That has the opposite effect on relationships. Differentiate your approach with the people you work with as you look for ways to integrate humor. That feels good to both people.

If you aren't naturally funny, find ways to make those on your team feel comfortable being funny themselves. Encourage the members of your team who have a well-received sense of humor by letting them know that you appreciate them and the impact that humor has on the team (if it's a good impact). If you are paying attention to this aspect as you are getting to know your people, you will find it is incredibly helpful for building easier and healthier relationships.

LAUGHTER BUILDS TRUST

But why should we laugh at work? One of the quickest ways to make those around you feel uncomfortable is to make a mistake and get really upset at yourself. What do they do at that point? Do they comfort you? Do they tell you how to fix it? Do they sit quietly while you seethe? The best way to deal with a situation like that is to put those around you at ease and laugh at yourself.

We've all been in the position where we have been embarrassed by something we have said or done. When confronted with that kind of discomfort, it's never easy to know what to do. Calling attention to what you did in a lighthearted way, and then making it right (apologizing, thinking through how you will do it differently with your team, etc.) can really give the people around you permission to feel comfortable with you. More importantly, they will begin to trust that you are not going to gloss over your own mistakes and that you will give them grace when they make them, as well.

In taking ownership for yourself and your behaviors, you are acknowledging that you have made a mistake and you are allowing them to acknowledge these things with you instead of behind your back. It also relieves any pressure that they might feel to "make you feel better" when you've made a mistake. Owning it and laughing about it, allows everyone to relax. All of this supports the creation of trust in relationships. Your colleagues will know that you are ok with making mistakes and that you will probably feel that way when they make mistakes, as long as they own their mistakes, as well.

LAUGHTER BUILDS RELATIONSHIPS

As the level of trust increases with your colleagues, you begin to build relational capacity together. Moments of laughter, because the brain retains those moments better in the memory, will create shared positive experiences that lead to easier conversation and ways for people to connect to each other. Ultimately, when people can laugh together, they learn that this relationship is safe and comfortable.

As you and your team are getting to know each other, you will begin to create a library of shared experiences. This happens naturally. If you are paying attention to ways that you can integrate humor, then you will begin to create inside jokes. Remembering these and thinking about ways to infuse these stories and jokes into stressful situations can help the entire team feel connected and supported.

Think of teams that you are a part of: your family of origin, your group of high school friends, your group of friends from college, a group of neighbors, your current family. Identify some of the things that each of these groups can laugh about no matter how many years have passed. When someone brings up a story that only this group remembers, what happens to you all?

If you are invested in this new place, you are working and in creating pathways for people to feel calmer and more at home, and curating these shared experiences is critical. These are the bonding moments that everyone in the group can rely on when times get difficult. If you have a hard time doing this, find someone on the team that is good at it, and encourage them to use that skill for the betterment of your entire team.

LAUGHTER DEFUSES CONFLICT

As your team grows together and their confidence around each other grows, humor can be a great tool to help with difficult conversations. A good leader knows that conflict is essential if the members of the team are going to move forward. Productive conflict in a psychologically safe environment helps all people think better and be more creative.

One of the ways to create more of that safety, is to notice when tensions are a little too high and diffuse it a bit with some humor. Either the self-deprecating kind that builds trust, or a shared joke, story or catch phrase. The time it takes for people to take a minute to acknowledge and laugh a bit, may give everyone in the room the break they need to process the discussion, think about their part and where they may go next.

After the giggling dies down, you as the leader can also remind the group of your bigger purpose, that you appreciate everyone being honest and that you want the team to remember that we can count on each other as we are working hard toward a bigger vision. That reassurance in the middle of conflict feels very comforting to people who may be getting tense or defensive. Laughter is healing. Teams who utilize it effectively can work more efficiently and productively together.

Finally, if you are a leader who laughs with their teams, you are giving permission for the other leaders to laugh with their teams. You are making it ok for your school and district to be a place where fun is encouraged. Because when it comes right down to it, students need to laugh. They need to feel safe when they make mistakes and they need to have fun with their teachers and with each other. That is how we make school a place they want to be, not have to be.

NOT EVERYTHING IS FUNNY

Many times, things that some people think are funny, are not funny to others. Without commenting on sensitivities, it is enough to say here that as a leader who is building relationships with your colleagues, it is of utmost importance that you check in with your team members regularly on whether they are feeling psychologically safe in your group. Bringing a sense of humility to these conversations, asking for their honest opinions and accepting the feedback they give is crucial. If the humor being utilized at the table is making *anyone* uncomfortable then it is not going to accomplish your goal of bringing people together and creating a sense of trust. This is a very delicate balance and one you need to pay attention to.

There are aspects of the *Wizard of Oz* that were funny when the movie was produced that have not "held up" over the years. Sensitivity to others should always be a top priority.

REFLECTION QUESTIONS FOR YOUR ACTION PLAN

- Who is the funniest person you know in your organization?
- Where does your organization already incorporate humor?

- Where can you strategically build in time to your team meetings for the team to watch, listen to, or share something humorous?
- Have there been times when you have discouraged humor or others have on your team, either implicitly or explicitly?
- Do you need to specifically tell your staff that humor is ok and appreciated?

SELF-MANAGEMENT PLANNING AND REFLECTION

- Are you building in time every once in a while, to explore a new place to find humor in your life? A new podcast, book, movie, TV show?
- Are there old friends that you can reconnect with who used to share humor with you and who could possibly help you cultivate more humor and joy in your life now?
- Are there aspects of your life that you have lost connection with, that if you reconnected, would give you more joy and opportunities to laugh?
- Have you explored values or beliefs that you have about humor at work or at home?
- Have others discouraged you from laughing or put down your sense of humor in the past?
- What types of humor do you appreciate most?

A RESOURCE FROM THE FIELD

Mary Kay Morrison gets into the science of using humor to help with learning in her book, Using Humor to Maximize Learning: The Links Between Positive Emotions and Education (Morrison 2007). In this book, you'll get some practical information on why humor matters for the brain to be at its best, how to exercise your humor muscles and how to recognize and avoid hurtful humor at all costs. This book is aimed at teachers and might be a powerful tool to support adults in your organization with seeing the benefits of kind humor to themselves and their students, ultimately helping everyone!

A RESOURCE FROM THE OUTFIELD

If you are looking to learn more about human behavior and how the brain works, the *Hidden Brain* podcast (Vedantham 2022) is going to be your best ally. Every week, Shankar Vedantham explores a new aspect of what motivates humans to act and think as they do and the consequences of those actions. The resources in this podcast are outstanding. The episodes are brief and almost always immediately applicable to your everyday life. The episodes on humor are fantastic and eye-opening for anyone looking to reap the benefits of laughter in life.

CASE STUDY ON LAUGHING WHEN THE WITCH IS ON YOUR TAIL: FINDING THE JOY

Situation

An experienced Superintendent arrived into her new district after the retirement of the previous leader. Upon beginning to ask questions and listen to her new colleagues, she found that the culture of the district was generally sad. Feelings of ineffectiveness were happening at most levels of the organization and some were blaming others for this feeling. Generally, relatively few people were taking ownership of their role or their impact on students in that role.

The previous leader was highly unsatisfied in the role and felt that he was not generally "cut out" for it after he was hired. He did the best he could, but he was really struggling to find meaning in the work, and generally felt that other leaders or teachers and staff shouldn't need that much support from him in order to be successful. He had been in the district for some time and felt that things were generally running the way they should, anyway.

The effects of this type of leadership were showing themselves in the apathy and general dissatisfaction of those around the new leader. Each day she walked around the buildings and sensed the tension or general discomfort and she knew there was no way they were going to be able to move forward together this way.

Overarching Challenge

This new leader needed to find a way to infuse joy and fulfillment into her new organization in a way that was not threatening and that helped to build relationships and a sense of hope and efficacy.

The Cost of Not Finding a Solution

A sad and uninspired workplace does not lead to productivity. If employees are feeling ineffective, a lack of ownership, and/or a sense of sadness and apathy, they will not be engaged at high levels, they will not be innovating and they will not be interested in continuous improvement. The cost of not creating a more satisfying and joyful workplace in schools, would be ultimately paid by the students and families by a lack of enthusiasm and dedication by the staff and teachers.

Solution

This new leader recognized early that one of the strong aspects of her personality could be useful in this situation. While she could see that many had been experiencing sadness, in each interaction where she could interject some humor or lightheartedness, it was received graciously and with relief. At first, she thought maybe this was just helping to break the ice, but she found that if she walked in each day and tried to find something happy, funny or interesting to talk with others about, that it began to change the culture.

Others would soon come into her office to share a funny story, or would include her when they were sharing things with each other. It became okay to laugh at work and to share celebrations. This had become almost a waste of time in the past, as eventually someone would bring up how terrible things were at work.

Slowly, she tried this when team discussions got difficult, as well. At first, this came in the form of self-deprecating humor. She found that when she opened up to her teams in a funny way with something that she has often struggled with, it became easier for her colleagues to do the same. Once they shared, it then became easier for her to support them or for them to support each other. Her humor was not "jokey" but more topical and sometimes sarcastic (but she was always careful with that kind of humor). Yet even without jokes, the team began to feel more at ease in the room with her and with each other.

This became a distinct feature of their office and meetings. There were rarely times when someone on the team couldn't ease tension or infuse some humor when it was needed. Of course, discussions on how to move forward and get refocused were sometimes difficult, but that's why the humor was so important. Each person on the team brought a different kind of "funny" to the table and the rhythm of interactions was fun and contagious. Ultimately, many people shared that it was fun to come to work again and that meant the world to the entire team.

Chapter 9

Share Your Kansas Stories

"You've always had the power my dear, you just had to learn it for yourself."

—*Glinda*

As Dorothy made her way through all the different parts of Oz, some of the sweetest moments of reflection for her were when she was thinking about her home in Kansas. The only home she ever knew before she landed in Oz, Kansas was where her story started. All of her new friends, surroundings and encounters were eventually compared to those people and places she left behind. Kansas made Dorothy who she was, and while she may have been feeling a bit curious about the rest of the world before the tornado, Kansas and all of her loved ones seemed very appealing by the end of her journey.

It's important as new leaders, especially as we work through discovering the nature of this new and chaotic place, to not forget our origins. The stories, experiences, successes, mistakes that we have had throughout our personal and professional lives have all made us who we are. They have shaped our opinions and values, our behaviors and attitudes and how we approach every, single day. To forget about those things, or ignore them, is to do a disservice to ourselves and those we are leading.

In an interview (Schawbel 2012) with *Forbes* magazine, Paul Smith, the author of *Lead with a Story: A Guide to Crafting Business Narratives that Captivate, Convince, and Inspire* (Smith 2012), Smith describes how seriously big corporations take storytelling as a way to lead effectively. He notes that some of the most successful companies in the world (like Microsoft and Nike) have corporate storytellers whose job it is to capture and share their most important stories, or teach storytelling skills explicitly to their executives.

Storytelling is how lessons are passed on, it's how relationships and connections are nurtured and its how empathy is cultivated. Sometimes people in chaotic organizations have gotten so comfortable with their own reality that they forget it doesn't have to be this way. Relating stories from your past and times that were simpler and more successful can create a vision for your people to attach to and look forward to. Ultimately, our goal is to bring peace and predictability to this volatile situation, and the next strategy for doing this, is to be relatable and share our stories.

CURATE YOUR STORIES

Journaling can have immense benefits in the area of gratitude and self-awareness. Taking time each day to write about our lives and reflect on our experiences can support finding patterns in our behavior, and our relationships and allow us to think through how we might adapt in the future to see better outcomes for ourselves and the ones we love. In terms of gratitude, journaling about the things we are thankful for can actually train our brain to find the positive aspects of life, which can ultimately impact our overall outlook and perspective.

There is another benefit to journaling for leaders, though, and this is the curation of our stories. School leaders are educators. The job of a school leader is to create a vision and communicate that purpose in a way that brings everyone into alignment around shared goals that will ultimately impact students in a positive way. In the creation of that vision and those goals, your stories can be very beneficial to help others understand what you are trying to communicate. The stories will give them an idea of where your vision and values originated from and help them anchor to you by understanding more about who you are. If you are looking for a quick way to get started on journaling, break out your old photo albums. Pictures are a great way to jump start your storytelling mind.

Knowing which stories are going to be beneficial at any point in the future is not important and actually isn't possible, which is even more reason to take time out of each day to record the stories that were most impactful to you, or someone around you. As you are documenting, think about what you learned through this situation and make a note of that somewhere outside of the text visually, so that later on you can refer to it and see quickly what stories you have available to you as you work to present your vision, goals, values, etc.

Or, utilize technology and create documents around big ideas that you already know you value: equity, belonging, productivity, efficiency, change, relationships, etc., and when you find yourself relating an experience to one of these values, document those stories right there in that section of your notes. Stories about students, teachers, parent interactions, Board conversions, and conference or workshop learnings are all great places to start with curating your stories.

Personal stories are very important here, as well. Stories about your children, parents, friends, pets, early work experiences, not only resonate with people as they are probably involved in some of these same types of relationships and situations, but they also reveal your humanity as a person who has a life outside of work. Stories about times you have failed, been embarrassed, created something new, taken a risk, can all be helpful as you coach and try to build relationships with those you are serving and leading with.

These stories will be helpful in your plans for communication. If you are writing a periodic newsletter or blog, or like to motivate and inspire those around you with weekly emails, or even as you are designing large presentations, having a journal full of stories and anecdotes creates a personal library for you to choose from when you don't have ideas readily available to you. If you are organizing your journal digitally, include photographs to help you remember the specifics or to illustrate an aspect of the story. You'll thank yourself later for the self-generated inspiration.

As you reread and review your own stories, you may find that they ground you personally too, as you work to maintain your humanity and untangle this new place. Remembering great times or times when things turned out well will help you stay calm as you try to bring people along with you to a calmer more peaceful reality.

FIND THE BOUNDARIES

Of course, not all of your stories are appropriate for sharing. Getting too personal or oversharing regarding your personal relationships or things you have struggled with at work or at home, can have the opposite effect than what you are looking for. Relating too many stories where things haven't worked as you thought they would might give people the impression that you aren't very good at making plans and achieving goals. Additionally, if you share these stories too early in your journey, you may not have established your credibility enough to withstand any judgement.

Your stories must also be relevant in some way to the work you are doing if shared in a professional setting, meeting or conversation. Getting off-topic for more than a couple of minutes can cause people to lose interest and feel that you are wasting their time telling them something that has no point to it. Sometimes sharing stories about new people you have met in an organization might feel to you like you are relating a funny or nice anecdote, for others, it might feel like gossip. Until you know how people respond to these types of stories, stick to the ones that are relevant to the work.

If you are sharing stories of things you are struggling with currently in a personal way, don't forget to consider how those around you may see you and your ability to lead being impacted by that situation. Leading as a victim of one's circumstances is not ideal. You don't want your people working with you and helping you because they feel sorry for you. That is a trap that causes resentment very quickly. Sharing struggles is fine if the point of it is to talk through how you are working to effectively resolve, learn more, collaborate, etc. on a solution. The listener should leave the situation feeling that you have a handle on what it is you are working through, and hopefully be reassured that it is alright for them to struggle as well, as long as they are moving forward.

Finally, and obviously, only share stories that are yours to share. If what you want to share with a group involves others in the group, check in with them first. Don't put anyone on the spot in the room by asking at that moment if you can share a story that might be embarrassing or even that might recognize them for something. Of course, don't ever share stories that others shared with you in confidence. It should go without saying, but if you don't know whether someone would want you to share it, don't share it until you ask them. If you have to tell someone that they cannot tell anyone else what you are about to tell them because it involves someone else, think twice or three times about sharing that story. You will make the listener question whether you can be trusted.

ENCOURAGE OTHERS TO SHARE

Through appropriate storytelling, your colleagues will hopefully become comfortable sharing their own stories. As they become more comfortable, think about including time in each of your staff meetings and agendas just for that purpose. The stories don't have to be shared with the whole group and not everyone needs to share every time, but offering the opportunity to think of and share stories is important so that people feel that their personal stories are just as important as yours. You might even consider creating opportunities for people to curate their own stories with respect to the goals of your organization by giving them advance notice of a topic for sharing or by creating online spaces for them to record their stories (with pictures, if possible).

For example, if you are going to be working on the change process with your staff, you might encourage your senior leadership team or teacher leaders to think through examples of when the change process was successful in their lives or in the school or district and when it wasn't. The reflection around that will lead to personal insights, the sharing will lead to good conversation and planning and ultimately, the entire team will wind up with more stories to "share forward" as you work with your staff.

TMI

If all this talk of sharing is making you or members of your team uncomfortable, here are some things to consider:

- What about sharing is uncomfortable? The length of time spent? The content? The responses that people have to the stories being shared?
- Before you arrived, was this a part of the culture?
- If not, does there need to be discussion on why storytelling can be a positive aspect of your organization?
- If it was part of the culture, was it productive and well-received?
- Are there still strong issues with trust among the team members that are prohibiting the sharing of stories being received well?
- Are the stories that are being shared contributing to the cultural issues of chaos inadvertently?

If this strategy seems to be backfiring or causing relationships to be more strained instead of stronger, have a discussion about that with your colleagues that you trust. Find a way to take a pause, and replace that activity with some learning experiences that will support your vision and mission more effectively that may still yield some of the same results. Some of those might include:

- Interest surveys to support people learning about each other
- Shared workspaces where questions are posed that provide people the opportunity to share opinions on a topic
- Book or podcast studies that provide people an opportunity to discuss something that might allow them to begin telling stories more easily in response to a specific question or prompt

REFLECTION QUESTIONS FOR YOUR ACTION PLAN

- Are there authors who can provide you with good stories that will also connect to your vision for your organization?
- Have you heard good stories about the organization already that can help you communicate your vision and values with stakeholders?

- Who are the best storytellers in the organization? Do they share their stories with everyone or just some people?
- Who has the most history in the organization? Can they help you curate some stories about where they have been?

SELF-MANAGEMENT PLANNING AND REFLECTION

- When you are telling or thinking about your personal stories, are there opportunities for you to learn more about yourself if you shared them with your counselor or coach?
- Who are the best storytellers in your life, and can you find some time to sit with them and hear some of their stories and learn how to become a better storyteller yourself?
- What kinds of stories resonate best with you as a learner? Funny? Heartwarming? Suspenseful? Ironic?
- Have you spent any time reflecting on your life story?
- Does your personal life story relate in any way to the journey that your district is on?
- What does it feel like when you share your personal stories with others?

A RESOURCE FROM THE FIELD

Laura Mitchell discusses how storytelling can help students find their value and a sense of belonging in their classroom. *Storytelling in a Culturally Responsive Classroom: Opening Minds, Shifting Perspectives and Transforming Imaginations* (Mitchell 2020) provides teachers with practical strategies for infusing storytelling into their classrooms. The goal of this type of storytelling is to gain additional perspectives and cultivate belonging.

By investing some time with this book, educational leaders will find out why storytelling can validate all aspects of those they are trying to lead, including your students, and how this strategy can be applied across the organization to model instruction that leads to a sense of belonging and connection.

A RESOURCE FROM THE OUTFIELD

The first podcasts/radio shows I ever listened to as an adult were from the show, *This American Life* (Glass 2022). This radio show is a treasure chest of stories around a theme. Each episode brings to life a concept through storytelling. The concept is simple however, the power is in seeing a concept through multiple perspectives. The podcast/show is enjoyable to listen to, and the stories and methods of storytelling can be instructive for those working to improve in this aspect of leadership.

 Also, remember that you don't need to have all your own stories to lead well. Stories from shows like this or other podcasts, books or movies can be just as powerful as your own stories. Many of these stories can be used as teaching tools for staff, students and families. The format of taking multiple perspectives on one topic can be useful for reflection in all areas of life and work.

CASE STUDY ON SHARING YOUR KANSAS STORIES: STORYTELLERS

Situation

A first-year principal was hired to begin in a year where all the elementary buildings in the district were being reorganized. In her new building, students from three different buildings were coming together to form a new school. In the spring before the new school year, she took the opportunity to come and meet her new community, as she was hired from outside the district. Over the summer, her assistant principal took another job out of the district, and she was assigned a new assistant principal, who had not yet finished her administrative degree, but who had worked as a teacher in the building for six years.

As the planning for the new year started to take place, the two new administrators realized that they were going to have quite a challenge bringing teachers and students from three different buildings together. The recognized that there might be differences in philosophy, culture, expectations, etc. They didn't really know what to expect, but were excited to begin.

It didn't take long for their fears to be realized. While teachers who came from the same building were getting along well, working with new folks was a challenge for almost every teacher. Every procedure from each building was different, down to ordering supplies. How to use parent volunteers, schedule field trips, get support with discipline, etc., were all difficult for everyone to navigate because this new administrative team was also coming from two very different experiences.

Simultaneously, within the first few weeks, the needs of the students were quickly taking over the space that they thought they had. More small spaces and offices were needed than the district had planned for, and the administrators were finding themselves moving staff around to accommodate. At some point in the first two months, the assistant principal even gave up her office and moved into the principal's office so that there could be one more space for small group instruction. At this point, the two were feeling frustrated and overwhelmed. Teachers were also feeling that way.

Overarching Challenge

Bring the staff members of this building together, and support the creation of a sense of community that ensures that everyone takes ownership of their new school.

The Cost of Not Finding a Solution

Blending school communities can be a difficult task as schools often have distinct cultures, processes, procedures and shared histories. While teachers could have continued to exist and thrive with the teachers they had known prior to this new school, eventually their discomfort around new colleagues would impact their ability to articulate across grade levels and disciplines.

Trying to allow each teacher to follow their own procedure or continue a practice that they "like" because it is what they've always done would certainly validate their experience, and maybe would help to create a sense of trust between that teacher and the administrator, but that would be eroded when everyone's systems bumped into each other and created more chaos and questions.

Finally, not being intentional about the creation of a new community through shared experiences would leave everyone feeling disconnected for a while. Leaving this kind of community building to chance is risky, as the more confident staff members from each school may take it upon themselves to make these opportunities, or they may not. And if they do, they might not involve those that they are not comfortable with.

A culture of belonging among teachers and administrators, a shared history and sense of efficacy is critical for ensuring that teachers feel confident, supported and happy at work. This will ultimately lead to better outcomes for students.

Solution

Sitting in their newly created double office, the two administrators began to thoughtfully develop plans to get the staff to know each other and have fun experiences that would lead to a new shared history. They planned faculty meetings to have time for people to discuss issues across teams, they planned staff outings and events, and they encouraged leaders from each building to share the things that they loved most about their previous building so that those aspects could be introduced in this new setting.

A critical component to this plan, although not planned at first, was that each of these experiences led to the creation of new stories. The principal was a gifted and engaging storyteller and would collect the stories from these interactions that staff were having over the course of the next couple of months. She would share and reshare the stories in various meetings and conversations and soon the staff were sharing these stories with each other. They became the narrative that the faculty were writing together. Because both administrators loved to laugh, the stories were often told with humor and ended with something positive that they were learning about their staff, students and families.

Culturally, this became the norm in a couple of years. Teachers and teams shared good new stories and highlighted them as celebrations of what was going right. The stories were also used to illustrate admiration for each other, or to show how much improvement someone had made. Creating the conditions for stories to emerge was key for bringing these staff members together to form a cohesive and engaged group of educators, dedicated to serving the needs of all students.

Chapter 10

Celebrate Before You Reach the Emerald City

"The dreams that you dare to dream, really do come true."

—*Dorothy*

Throughout this book we have discussed that the goal of leading a school or district through chaos is to ultimately find a pathway forward to a more calm and stable organization that is focused on what students need. You have worked to ensure that you are a good listener, planner, collaborator and colleague. You have shared a lot about yourself and have learned a lot about those around you. Through those conversations, many have shared what they need from you and the organization that they are not getting. These needs may or may not be connected to the priority areas you have identified and may or may not be aligned to your vision for the organization.

Leaders are often taught to gather information upon entering an organization so that you can gain some "quick wins." The idea behind this philosophy is that quick wins build your credibility as a leader who listens, responds and accomplishes goals quickly. These wins can provide more than that, though, they can provide an opportunity for newly formed teams to celebrate together and in turn, create more momentum for moving forward.

The problem with quick wins in a chaotic organization is that since there is no alignment and no vision, changing anything quickly can add to the chaos. The solution may provide relief to some people, but others may find it confusing or upsetting. Choosing whose issues to address may also lead some to believe that you are creating alliances with some people and not others. Quick wins are great for providing a reason to celebrate success early. But be mindful, there will be many opportunities to celebrate as you move forward on the path to your goal. Relying on quick wins right now for those celebrations, may not be the wisest move.

STAY FOCUSED

As you and your team become clearer about how your organization is struggling and what you intend to do about it, ensure that every decision is in alignment with that. At the beginning, it may feel to some people like you are not doing enough. Some people will be frustrated at your lack of resolution to their problems. But if you are being transparent and keeping your process open as we have discussed, there will also be times that your people are relieved that you have not jumped to fix something based on one or two pieces of feedback and without understanding the whole context.

When the team decides that there is a way to solve a problem that won't create more problems and that is in alignment with your assessment and plans, that is the time to implement that solution, make it public and celebrate the end results. When you do get that party started, keep the celebration focused on the fact that this is just one step in getting everyone to the bigger goal. Keep the celebration small and keep focusing on the fact that there is a lot more work to do together. Remind people that you will be gathering more information in order to move forward and accomplish more goals.

Understand that celebration of any small or quick win can be perceived by some in a chaotic organization to be wasted time. They may not like their colleagues at all and may find spending any kind of "joyful" time together to be annoying. Some may see these early celebrations as self-promotion or an example of lack of self-awareness on your part. Some may see celebrations as just low on the list of priorities when there is so much work to do to get back to focusing on students. Remember, there is little to no trust when you walk into a chaotic place and although you are working to build it, no one wants to work for a leader who is clueless to big problems and just looks for opportunities to make people happy at any cost.

Individuals may also really still be struggling with the bigger cultural issues that you have identified and reminding them that there are some problems being resolved, while theirs isn't, is not welcome information. Recognition of small successes is important, though, as you need people to know that you are all moving forward in a good direction but that you recognize there is a long way to go.

RESEARCH THE CELEBRATION CULTURE

Not everyone likes to celebrate the same way. If you are going to be recognizing the contributions of people in the organization, make sure you know that those people are comfortable with how they will be recognized and that culturally, you are not going to be setting the organization back. Ask your senior leadership team about how celebrations have been approached in the past and be intentional about what your plans will be moving forward. Ask your people how they like to be recognized or if they even want to be. This shows that you are aware that one size does not fit all in this area.

Think of new ways to recognize small successes that will be unique to your journey together. Allow others to join into nominating people or solutions for recognition and be thoughtful about who is getting recognized and how often. Always, as the leader, keep the recognition focused on the ways that it will bring about change that is needed on a bigger scale and that will ultimately lead to the end results you are collectively looking to achieve.

If you are finding that people are just not liking the idea of celebrating anything, celebrate the achievements of your students. There are not many educators that will look the other way when recognizing the hard work and efforts of the children that they are working with. Solicit the input of your administrators and teachers to find the children who are really doing outstanding things and make those celebrations the focal point of your recognition efforts, until you have a sense of how the adults would feel comfortable recognizing their own efforts toward a more calm and focused school or district.

CELEBRATE REAL WINS

In this new setting, especially in the beginning of your journey, there will be many who will not agree that anything you celebrate is actually a win. As has been discussed, there are many reasons that your new home has been or is in chaos right now. Some of the reasons might be that people have *chosen* to continue the chaos. Although that doesn't make sense intuitively, it is true that chaos is beneficial in some ways. A chaotic environment:

- Hides lack of skill or knowledge
- Prevents forward movement and change
- Creates alliances (an in-group and an out-group)
- Allows for independence
- Diffuses focus

While many people in the organization, or those who are served by the organization may say they desperately want a more functioning and focused environment, some of them probably feel more at home in the chaos that exists and are fearful that any change will result in a loss of connections with some of their alliances and their own independence. They may also correctly predict that it will result in increases in accountability and focus.

As you begin to celebrate anyone's successes, remember that each one needs to be framed in a way that redefines an aspect of the organization as beneficial to as many stakeholder groups as possible. By doing so, you are encouraging *everyone* to stick with you through this journey. The people in the organization who want the change and are not afraid of your vision for the future will be your champions and will be helping you plan these celebrations.

Those who want the change but are fearful of its impact on them, need to see you celebrating *with* them, not *against* them, for them to begin participating more in the change process. Those who don't want the change at all will begin to see that if they stay, they will need to get on board with the bigger group or they will lose their alliances all together because they are not willing to celebrate and champion a more effective and more functional working environment and culture.

CELEBRATE WITH DATA

No matter what, ensure to the greatest degree possible that the celebration is actually highlighting a real success. If it is not, it will be defined as toxic positivity. Toxic positivity has been highlighted as a real issue in organizations recently. It is evident when leaders try to convince people that everything can be reframed in a positive light. Even situations where the outcome is devastating, are spun to find the silver lining.

This kind of obsession with celebration and optimism causes people to ignore their actual emotions and feel pressured to act happy and have fun, even when that is the last thing they are feeling. This creates resentment and will further erode the trust and psychologically safe environment that you are focused on creating. We know as leaders that optimism is important and that we should highlight our successes. But there are ways to do it and avoid being toxic about it.

Use data and evidence to support that each change is making a positive difference. Have others share anecdotally how it has impacted them or their students and families in a positive way. Be sure to highlight the contributions of everyone who is making the change possible. Outline all the work it took to get to the point where you have seen results. Detail who will continue to champion this change and how you will sustain or scale it up in the future.

By framing your celebrations in this way, you are modeling for your staff that it is healthy to recognize achievements and that when there is evidence to show that you are making a difference, it can be a powerful tool for creating more momentum forward. You are also demonstrating that you are not there to promote yourself, your work or their work, no matter what the outcome. You are looking for authentic ways to detail your successes. This creates trust in you as a leader as someone who can be relied upon to tell the real story when things are going right, and when things are not.

REFLECTION QUESTIONS FOR YOUR ACTION PLAN

- Who makes up the "cheer section" of your organization and have you included them in your planning?
- Have you talked with these folks about how to ensure that we are not advocating for a toxically optimistic environment?
- Have celebrations been overused or not used at all here in the past?
- How can you make these new celebrations unique and special, while still honoring the past successes and celebrations of the organization?

SELF-MANAGEMENT PLANNING AND REFLECTION

- How do celebrations at work resonate with you as a person?
- Have you ever been a part of a celebration that didn't feel authentic? What response did you have for that?
- When you consider celebrating the wins you are seeing, do they feel authentic and do you have evidence to show that they are actually wins?
- Have you personally ever worked for someone who only celebrated the achievements that were made after their arrival and never the things that went right before they arrived? How did that feel?
- Do you need help in the celebration department?
- Where in your personal life do you take time to celebrate your accomplishments or the accomplishments of your loved ones?
- If you have trouble with celebrating, why is that? Where did that come from?

A RESOURCE FROM THE FIELD

In *Step In, Step Up,* Jane Kise and Barbara Watterson (Watterson 2019) explore how being female in leadership can at times create a double-bind experience of adhering to both traditionally male and female gender expectations. Celebrations and "cheerleading" can often feel like a traditionally female role, and exploring this aspect of your personality and leadership as you are working to incorporate this into your leadership journey, may help ease some of the frustrating impacts that others' expectations can have on your plans and any attacks on your reputation.

A RESOURCE FROM THE OUTFIELD

In the podcast, *Unf*ck Your Brain* (Lowentheil 2022), Kara Lowentheil explores issues of anxiety, self-doubt and imposter phenomenon for high-achieving women. The many issues discussed in this podcast help to break down the social constructs that specifically impact women and support the achievement of goals, including managing one's own mind.

Again, as a female leader in a still predominantly male environment, it is important to understand your own mind as you seek to decide what is worth celebrating for yourself for others and on your personal leadership journey. There will be many times that you will question yourself on what you have really been able to achieve and whether you should be recognizing those achievements. This podcast can help with those self-doubts (for males, too) and provide practical strategies for overcoming any confidence issues that are certain to arise in a chaotic leadership experience. If you are uncomfortable with profanity, this podcast may not be for you.

Chapter 11

Realize Oz Is About More Than Just the Wizard, It's About the Journey

"Experience is the only thing that brings knowledge."

—Frank L. Baum

The process of leading an organization through the storm of chaos and dysfunction is a journey you will never forget. The events will fade, but the feelings, emotions and relationships made will live forever inside of you. As difficult a journey as it is, the learning that comes from this type of school leadership is priceless. There is no amount of professional development or coursework that can provide this level of growth.

For the organization itself, the process is painful. It is full of uncertainty and questioning and can lead many in the organization to become frustrated and question themselves and their place in the world, regularly. Change takes everyone's attention, it is impacted by everyone and it impacts everyone. As vision and clarity begin to emerge, as the storm dies down and the sun starts to shine, there will be a collective sense of accomplishment and renewed purpose. Moving forward will finally feel good.

When that day comes, it is important to help everyone see how far they have come, and to recognize the tremendous efforts of everyone in getting to the point where they can focus back on doing what is right for students in their classrooms. Similar to the way a student or teacher might create a portfolio throughout a unit of study, gathering evidence of your change process can be helpful in assessing how you are doing individually, collectively and inform your next steps.

Documentation like this is important because at many points in your process, you will lose your way. Chaos is disorienting, and it turns you around.

Sometimes you lose your North Star. Documenting and reflecting on your journey will help you to keep clear about where you have been, what it is you have been trying to accomplish and remind you that you *are* somewhere new, even if it's not exactly where you need to be yet.

DEVELOP A SYSTEM FOR DOCUMENTATION

Listening, being transparent about your process, celebrating when there have been successes, sharing your stories with each other. Utilizing each of these strategies can yield a treasure trove of artifacts. Notes, pictures, videos, meeting minutes, and recordings can later serve you as you reflect for and with others in the organization about how the change process occurred. As soon as you can, find simple ways to organize these snapshots of your process in a way that can be easily accessed in the future.

Create shared folders online with big themes and drop into them evidence that illustrates the work you are doing. Or organize the artifacts chronologically to give you a way to "see" where you have been and how far you've come. Online bulletin boards are a good way to do this, too. In this format, it is easy to remind people using digital sticky notes, what you are learning, quotes that remind you of conversations, resources you have used, etc. Think about ways that you can creatively entice your team to participate in this.

ENCOURAGE OTHERS TO CONTRIBUTE

Build in time with your team to collect: photos, stories, memos that help to illustrate your journey in whatever way you have decided to organize the information. Thinking about the process from multiple perspectives is enlightening and can really highlight the complexities of your work. Although minute details are easily forgotten, it is in the small moments that we sometimes find the most powerful impact. When you make space for collecting evidence of particular parts of your journey during your time together, you create more shared experiences. You also demonstrate that you value each member of your team and how they contribute to and see your journey. You are also modeling that the learning doesn't come at the end of the process, unit of instruction, etc. The learning takes place throughout the journey.

REFLECT ON THE PROCESS

Just as you build in time to collect evidence of your process, make time for your team to strategically revisit the steps you have taken to move from a chaotic system to a more focused system. Have intentional debriefing sessions where you discuss what has worked, what hasn't worked well and why. Think about the types of resources or strategies that you have used and what has been the most effective. Take time to think about how that information can be applied to current situations and decisions that you are grappling with as a team.

Encourage your teams to do this with the teams that they lead. As the lead learner in a learning organization, it is your responsibility to be the master teacher. The goal of your work should always be to model the most effective strategies for learning, assessing, reflecting and applying new knowledge. Participating in this type of work may feel like "busy work" for some folks who don't like to spend a lot of time looking in the rearview mirror. Those people may need some coaching to be reminded of what your purpose is and that is continuous improvement. Making the same mistakes over and over because you have missed opportunities to document, assess and reflect is a waste of everyone's time.

REFLECTION QUESTIONS FOR YOUR ACTION PLAN

- Have you encountered documentation of any journeys this organization has been on before you arrived?
- Is there someone on your team that likes to document: take pictures, write follow-up emails, create videos, etc.?
- Can you find someone to be that type of documentarian to not only help with making space for this work, but also help you find places where that kind of documentation can be impactful to your organization?

SELF-MANAGEMENT PLANNING AND REFLECTION

- Have you ever been included in a montage of photos or video that is celebrating or remembering someone or something?
- How did it feel to see yourself or your work in that reflection?
- Are there areas of your personal life that you are good at documenting and areas where you shy away from it?

- Is there someone in your life who is very good at that and if so, can they support you with new, fun ways to do it?

A RESOURCE FROM THE FIELD

Professional Learning Communities at Work and High Reliability Schools (Robert Eaker 2020) is a powerhouse of a resource for any school or district leader looking to create a culture of continuous improvement and collaboration in their school district. The authors offer practical strategies for addressing common issues found in schools and districts across the country and how to build systems that make the right decisions for students.

A RESOURCE FROM THE OUTFIELD

In his podcast *Revisionist History* (Gladwell 2022), Malcolm Gladwell takes a deep dive into situations or people who have been overlooked or misunderstood. Ultimately, the big idea of this podcast is that every situation deserves rethinking and reflection. Although the stories are interesting and engaging on their own, leaders may find lessons in here that help reframe their own thoughts when things don't go as planned. It's funny, too.

Chapter 12

"Remember, there's no place like home"

Back in sepia tone, back in her bed, back with her family and friends, Dorothy's chaotic journey of leadership had ended. She took her new friends on the journey of their lives, through danger and excitement, through mystery and discovery and they had all received what they were after. When she learns that all she needed to do was click her ruby slippers together and wish for home, she does so, but not before she bids her friends goodbye and recognizes all they taught her on the journey and how much she will miss them. Her next steps are unclear for certain, but she definitely has learned about herself and her values through the process. It's a truly warm, comforting and happy conclusion.

Some have viewed Dorothy's as a Hero's Journey. This common narrative structure is embraced throughout the world as one of the most satisfying ways to tell a compelling story because of its basic three parts: The Departure Phase, the Initiation Phase and the Return Phase. It can be argued that this is any leader's journey and that leading an organization through chaos successfully is truly a heroic act. You have left a world you knew and were successful in, you have heeded the call for adventure and purpose. You have found mentors, obstacles, tests, allies, and enemies, and eventually, you have found a new home that embraces you and the many sacrifices you have made for those you serve.

The journey of any school leader will always ultimately be about bringing resources and alignment to a system in order to improve outcomes for students. You will work with teachers, paraprofessionals, parents, community members, and hopefully the students themselves, to understand the obstacles to achievement and growth that are present and find ways to work together to remove those obstacles. When the system you are leading is in crisis and chaos, there is one resource that is imperative to the first stage of the journey. That resource is connection.

These ten strategies for leading through crises are ultimately all about connection. Connection to oneself, to others, to the organization in meaningful, authentic, and impactful ways. Connection heals hurt and transforms lives. By creating these connections, a leader can help weave a human safety net that stands at the ready when systems fail and people lose their way. Connections to each other, to mission, vision, purpose and shared history, are the strong threads that will keep this safety net intact.

The journey through chaos toward common vision, mission and goals isn't linear. It is important to remember that even as the system becomes more aligned and productive, chaos will always have opportunities to reappear. Sometimes those opportunities will come through external factors, and sometimes internally, the chaos will be ushered back in by those who are afraid of the movement you are making.

Unfortunately, sometimes chaos is embraced by many people as armor. Chaos and constant crisis can protect people from accountability at any level of any organization or in any situation. The more variables there are affecting the outcome, the more that anyone can point outward when things go wrong to one or many parts of the "system" that failed, and shield themselves and their actions by simply saying, "I don't know about anything else, but I know I am doing what I am supposed to do." It is apparent in the world right now, that chaos exists everywhere and that sometimes, it exists on purpose.

For the school leader who genuinely wants to make change, who truly wants to support a functional and effective organization that is doing the right things for all of its students, she will have to be vigilant that chaos doesn't continue to creep back into the system. She will have to consistently evaluate systems, processes and organizational structure to ensure that the organization doesn't just become more organized chaos, still devoid of accountability and real impact on the lives of students. More isn't always better: more processes, more forms, more systems, more meetings. In fact, those aspects of working in a school or district can overwhelm people just as much as the lack of them can. Forgetting the old adage, keep it simple, stupid, would be a mistake.

It takes courage to step into a position of leadership. Whether you are taking control of your own life and becoming your own hero or whether you are taking a step beyond that and making the decision to lead others, courage is critical and it always has been. However, taking on public and formal leadership roles in the field of education, especially in this particular time in our history, feels a lot more dangerous and full of peril than it ever has.

Not only is one agreeing to be responsible for others and accountable for outcomes, leadership of schools and districts requires a skin thick enough to withstand public battles that you may not even know are happening in your own community, you may not know you are involved in, and in which you cannot and should not actively participate. The public school leader now needs to have a presence that reaches far beyond her physical domain and is accessible to individuals she may not even know that she affects. Social media is often the battleground where leadership is attacked. School leaders need to be able to withstand those attacks with courage and perseverance.

Some people approach educational leadership with a determination to not let anyone or anything affect or change them. That is understandable and perhaps the most sane response to the sometimes irrational treatment of these leaders. However, taking that guarded stance and sticking with such firm resolve to who one is at the beginning of a hero's journey, can result in a steep downfall. To use a new metaphor, skyscrapers are built to sway in the storm. They are meant to withstand the wind by being flexible. They shift and bend, so they do not break. They stand taller than anything around them, even in the middle of the storm.

Because of the various waves of educational reform that have hit schools in the last 30 years, oftentimes priorities of educational leaders shift as they collaborate with their communities. But these efforts to problem solve can be attacked from within school districts by teachers and staff who have "seen everything before." Or, it can be seen as a sign of weakness and "giving in" to parents or boards of education. To school leaders trying to stand firm but flexibly, leadership can feel like a completely lose-lose proposition.

Leaders are often criticized as "weak minded" when they are continuing to learn, collaborating with others, or changing their opinion at times. It can be similarly challenging to answer the accusation that shifting opinions or direction indicates a lack of preparation or resolve. The truth is though, that leading as a learner of oneself and others is the strongest type of leadership. And leading schools in this way should be seen as the ideal model, as we know that this is exactly the kind of learners and leaders we need our students to be.

The curious, vulnerable and thoughtful leader will stand in storms and bend, but not break. She will move and shift when she needs to, she will learn her environment and eventually bring calm through her ability to bring the eye of the storm to her, so that she can hear the signals sent in the distance and lead others to a better place.

The "loudest" critics of these types of transformational leaders are those sitting, protected by their glass screens, shouting their opinions through their fingertips. They cut, paste, crop, and spin in order to keep the chaos going and they don't even watch for the leader to fail, but instead for how others will react to their comments and opinions. A heart, or a thumbs up, moments that will be logged for a second by a glance in a stranger's memory, becomes the fuel for their never-ending obsession with having something to say. That feedback loop will leave them continually thirsting for more affirmation and never actually fulfilled. Those folks are not the storm but they do contribute to the climate, if we let them.

Now more than ever, school leaders need to step into all the storms and listen to those who are impacted most by it, not those who are the loudest observers of the storm. Students have experienced the storms firsthand. Courageous leaders who are willing to be in the storm with them and bring their communities together for positive change that will impact their lives, are the solution to many of our issues in education. This change can happen in families, in neighborhoods, in communities, in schools and districts, and in nations if we want it to. If our students experience leadership like this, they might just choose to be leaders when they grow up. Young leaders can do this work now. Young women also have this power.

While change is constant and can often feel like chaos, leaders can use the tools presented here to bring order to the change process and ensure clarity through what could feel like chaos, but doesn't have to. There is a lot of chaos happening around us in the world. We can each choose to help lead our small corner of it. Sometimes this is within ourselves, in our homes, in our offices, or in our communities, but most certainly in our schools. We can lead with integrity, with humor, with authenticity, and with curiosity in a way that can bring connection, abundance, calm, peace and belonging to everyone we encounter. There truly is no place like that kind of home and no other type of home that should be left to our children.

Bibliography

Brown, Brené. 1st edition 2021. *Atlas of the Heart: Mapping Meaningful Connection and the Language of Human Experience.* Random House.

Brown, Brené (Host). 2020. *Dare to Lead* [Audio Podcast]. Parcast.

Burden, Gay, and Stu Siblerman. 2019. *Asking the Right Questions: A Guide to Continuous Improvement with Stakeholder Input.* Rowman & Littlefield Publishers.

Bush, Lynn, and Howard Bultinck. 1st edition 2013. *99 Ways to Lead and Succeed.* Routledge.

Calm. 2021. *Calm App.* Accessed May 9, 2022.

Oxford's English Dictionaries. 2022. *Oxford Languages.* Accessed May 9, 2022. www.languages.oup.com.

Doyle, Glennon (Host). 2021. *We Can Do Hard Things* [Audio Podcast].

Eaker, Robert, Robert J. Marzano, and Mario Acosta. 2020. *Professional Learning Communities at Work and High Reliability Schools TM: Cultures of Continuous Learning (Ensure a viable and guaranteed curriculum).* Solution Tree Press.

Fleming, Victor (Director). 1939. *The Wizard of Oz* [Film]. Metro-Goldwyn-Mayer.

Gladwell, Malcolm (Host). 2022. *Revisionist History* [Audio Podcast]. Pushkin Industries.

Glass, Ira. 2022. *This American Life.* WBEZ Radio and PRX.

Grant, Adam (Host). 2022. *WorkLife with Adam Grant: A TED Original Podcast* [Audio Podcast].

Hobson, Neville, and Shel Holtz (Hosts). 2022. *For Immediate Release* [Audio Podcast]. FIR Podcast Network.

Kruse, Kevin. 2022. "Articles." *Lead X.* Accessed May 9, 2022. https://leadx.org/articles/what-is-authentic-leadership/.

Lowentheil, Kara. 2022. *Unf*ck Your Brain.* KL Coaching. https://unfuckyourbrain.com.

Mayo Clinic Staff. 2021. "Stress Relief from Laughter? It's no joke." *Mayo Clinic.* Accessed May 9, 2022. www.mayoclinic.org.

Mitchell, Laura. 2020. *Storytelling in a Culturally Responsive Classroom: Opening Minds, Shifting Perspectives and Transforming Imaginations.* Lexington.

Morrison, Mary Kay. 2007. *Using Humor to Maximize Learning: The Links Between Positive Emotions and Education.* Rowman & Littlefield Publishers.

Nahum-Shani, Inbal, et al. 2014. "Supervisor support: Does supervisor support buffer or exacerbate the adverse effects of supervisor undermining?" *Journal of Applied Psychology 99*(3), 484–503.

National Institute for Health and Welfare. 2020. "Science News." *Science Daily.* Accessed May 9, 2022. www.sciencedaily.com.

NSPRA. n.d. *National School Public Relations Association.* Accessed May 9, 2022. www.nspra.org.

Oxford's English Dictionaries. 2022. *Oxford Languages.* Accessed May 9, 2022. www.languages.oup.com.

Perel, Esther (Host). 2019. *How's Work? with Esther Perel* [Audio Podcast]. Global Media and Gimlet.

Polyak, Nick, and Michael Lubelfeld. 2017. *The Unlearning Leader: Leading for Tomorrow's Schools Today.* Rowman & Littlefield Publishers.

Rodberg, Simon. 2020. *What If I'm Wrong? and Other Key Questions for Decisive School Leadership.* ASCD.

Schawbel, Dan. 2012. "How to Use Storytelling as a Leadership Tool." *Forbes*, August 13. https://www.forbes.com/sites/danschawbel/2012/08/13/how-to-use-storytelling-as-a-leadership-tool/?sh=34d3873a5e8e

Smith, Paul. 2012. *Lead with a Story: A Guide to Crafting Business Narratives the Captivate, Convince and Inspire.* AMACOM.

Thomas, Maura. 2018. "4 Ways Leaders Can Protect Their Time and Empower Their Employees." *Harvard Business Review*, July 18. https://hbr.org/2018/07/4-ways-leaders-can-protect-their-time-and-empower-their-teams

TINYpulse. 2013. *7 Vital Trends Disrupting Today's Workplace Results and Data from 2013 TINYpulse Employee Engagement Survey.* Engagement Survey, TINYpulse.

Vedantham, Shankar. 2022. *Hidden Brain.* Hidden Brain Media.

Warwick, Ronald. 2014. *The Challenge for School Leaders: A New Way of Thinking about Leadership.* Rowman & Littlefield Publishers.

Watterson, Barbara, and Jane Kise. 2019. *Step In, Step Up: Empowering Women for the School Leadership Journey (A 12 Week Educational Leadership Development Guide for Women).* Solution Tree Press.

Wells, Caryn. Reprint Edition 2016. *Mindfulness: How School Leaders can Reduce Stress and Thrive on the Job.* Rowman & Littlefield Publishers.

Wise, Robert (Director). 1965. *The Sound of Music* [Film]. Argyle Enterprises, Inc.

Worthington, Everett. 2020. "How hope can keep you healthier and happier." *The Conversation.* Accessed May 9, 2022. www.theconversation.com.

About the Author

Lisa Leali has been Superintendent of Schools for Lake Bluff Elementary School District 65 since July 2020. She has over 20 years of experience in public education as an elementary school teacher, assistant principal, coordinator for curriculum and technology, director of teaching and learning and as an assistant superintendent for curriculum and instruction.

Lisa earned her master's degree in Educational Leadership in 2007 from Northeastern Illinois University and her doctorate in Educational Leadership in 2010 from National-Louis University. Her dissertation was titled "Joyful Classrooms, Successful Kids: A Study in the Connection Between Joy and Learning." She has served as a consultant for school districts on standards-based reporting and writing instruction, has presented regionally on data and assessment and has presented nationally on the topic of instructional coaching. She currently serves on the Partnership Board for the Northeastern Illinois University Principal Endorsement Program.

www.ingramcontent.com/pod-product-compliance
Lightning Source LLC
Chambersburg PA
CBHW030143240426
43672CB00005B/241